Praise f

Recovery, the 12 Steps an
Reclaiming Hope, Courage & Wholeness

"I can't recall a book that has opened my eyes, touched my heart or awakened my soul more than Paul Steinberg's *Recovery, the 12 Steps and Jewish Spirituality*. If you measure this treasure in terms of insight, honesty, courage and compassion, it matches the greatest works of the human soul. I will be sharing this book widely, and returning to it again and again."
> —**Rabbi Bradley Shavit Artson, DHL**, vice president,
> American Jewish University; author, *Passing Life's Tests:*
> *Spiritual Reflections on the Trial of Abraham, the Binding of Isaac*

"Rabbi Steinberg has written the go-to resource for Jews in recovery, and also for those who wish to support them. His honesty about his own addiction and recovery, combined with his insights into Jewish spiritual teachings, make this a very powerful book—comforting and inspiring as well as informative and accessible. The wisdom of Jewish tradition and of the 12 Steps are brought together here in ways that deepen our understanding of both."
> —**Louis E. Newman**, John M. and Elizabeth W. Musser
> Professor of Religious Studies, Carleton College;
> author, *Repentance: The Meaning and Practice of Teshuvah*

"It takes a courageous soul to stand naked and bare one's soul in the public square. Rabbi Steinberg has done just that in *Recovery, the 12 Steps and Jewish Spirituality*. His remarkable candor … will surely enlighten and empower others who … struggle with addiction, perfectionism, Judaism and spirituality…. [He] has taken the complex challenges of understanding addiction, recovery, God, honesty, AA, *mitzvot*, spirituality, love, Judaism, trust, Torah and humanity and woven them into a seamless tapestry. I am grateful to Rabbi Steinberg for sharing himself through the book, and for the many new insights I gleaned from its pages."
> —**Janice Kamenir-Reznik**, cofounder and president,
> Jewish World Watch

RECOVERY, the 12 STEPS and JEWISH SPIRITUALITY

Reclaiming Hope, Courage & Wholeness

Rabbi PAUL STEINBERG

Foreword by Rabbi Abraham J. Twerski, MD

Preface by Harriet Rossetto

For People of All Faiths, All Backgrounds

JEWISH LIGHTS Publishing

Woodstock, Vermont

www.jewishlights.com

Recovery, the 12 Steps and Jewish Spirituality:
Reclaiming Hope, Courage & Wholeness

2014 Quality Paperback Edition, First Printing
© 2014 by Paul Steinberg
Foreword © 2014 by Abraham J. Twerski
Preface © 2014 by Harriett Rossetto

For information regarding permission to reprint material from this book, please mail or fax your request in writing to Jewish Lights Publishing, Permission Department, at the address / fax number listed below, or e-mail your request to permissions@jewishlights.com.

Library of Congress Cataloging-in-Publication Data
Steinberg, Paul, 1973– author.
  Recovery, the 12 steps and Jewish spirituality : reclaiming hope, courage & wholeness / Rabbi Paul Steinberg ; foreword by Rabbi Abraham J. Twerski, MD ; preface by Harriet Rossetto.
      pages cm
  Includes bibliographical references.
  ISBN 978-1-58023-808-3 — ISBN 978-1-58023-816-8 (ebook) 1. Steinberg, Paul, 1973- 2. Jews—Alcohol use—United States—Attitudes. 3. Jews—Alcohol use. 4. Alcoholism—Religious aspects—Judaism. 5. Twelve-step programs—Religious aspects—Judaism. 6. Spiritual life—Judaism. I. Title.
  HV5185.S74 2014
  296.3'8—dc23
                            2014027023

10 9 8 7 6 5 4 3 2 1
Manufactured in the United States of America
Cover design: Mike Myers
Interior design: Tim Holtz

For People of All Faiths, All Backgrounds
Published by Jewish Lights Publishing
A Division of LongHill Partners, Inc.
Sunset Farm Offices, Route 4, P.O. Box 237
Woodstock, VT 05091
Tel: (802) 457-4000   Fax: (802) 457-4004
www.jewishlights.com

"In the view of The Holy Blessed One, one who has sinned and repented has a higher status than one who has never sinned."

—Rabbi Moses Cordovero

"One of the disconcerting—and delightful—teachings of the master was: 'God is closer to sinners than saints.' This is how he explained it: 'God in heaven holds each person by a string. When you sin, you cut the string. Then God ties it up again, making a knot—and thereby bringing you a little closer to him. Again and again your sins cut the string—and with each further knot God keeps drawing you closer and closer.'"

—Anthony De Mello

Contents

Foreword

Many years ago I began a personal campaign to alert the Jewish community that Jews can be alcoholic. The resistance was formidable. The myth *"shikker is a goy"* (a drunkard is a gentile) was solidly entrenched. Very gradually, the resistance began to erode, but the severity of the stigma, the *shonde* (disgrace) factor, causes the myth to persist. Rabbi Paul Steinberg's masterful *Recovery, the 12 Steps and Jewish Spirituality* may finally put this dangerous myth to rest.

Then I found much resistance to the 12 Step program of Alcoholics Anonymous because of its origin in the Christian Oxford Group. Buttressed by the common meeting place of AA in church basements—because synagogues did not welcome them!—the feeling was that AA is a Christian program and is off-limits for Jews. My assertion that Bill Wilson must have plagiarized the works of *mussar* (Jewish ethics) has not eliminated this misconception.

Rabbi Steinberg's explanation of the identity of the 12 Steps with Jewish spirituality is greatly enhanced by his personal reflections. Some serious Torah students, thoroughly familiar with *mussar*, have fallen victim to addiction and have recovered with AA. The question is, why was AA effective when *mussar* was not?

Rabbi Steinberg's personal reflections provide the answer to this question. When a person who is sincere in recovery leaves an AA meeting, he or she has a gut feeling, "If I deviate from this program, I die." The person who studies *mussar* may believe intellectually, "This is indeed an excellent way to live a spiritual life," but does not have a gut feeling that his or her very life is dependent on total adherence to the program, and that any deviation from it is certain death.

Rabbi Steinberg's personal reflections reveal his awareness that for him, and for every addict, the 12 Steps are the oxygen without which a person cannot live.

One of the important similarities between AA and Jewish spirituality is the statement in Step 12, "to practice these principles in all our affairs." The Talmud says, "Which is the small verse upon which the entire Torah is dependent? 'Know [God] in all your ways'" (Proverbs 3:6, Berachot 63a).

Judaism repudiates the idea of "Give to Caesar what is to Caesar and to God what is to God" (Matthew 22:21). There is no dichotomy of sacred versus secular. The principles of Torah apply not only to performance of the mitzvot but also to all of our actions. Jewish spirituality applies to how we eat, sleep, work, socialize, and recreate. There is nothing that is external to the relationship of human being to God.

It is a mistake to think that the 12 Steps are targeted toward alcohol, drugs, gambling, or sex. Practicing the principles of the 12 Steps in "all our affairs" mirrors the dictum "know [God] in all your ways." Anyone who limits exercising the 12 Steps to his or her addiction has a very shallow recovery.

It is unfortunate that only addicts can avail themselves of the 12 Step program. Rabbi Steinberg shows that a proper understanding of Jewish spirituality enables everyone to achieve the personal growth and transformation that is so effective in reversing a lifestyle that is so common, of going full speed ahead to nowhere.

—Rabbi Abraham J. Twerski, MD

Preface

In the film *Keeping the Faith*, the rabbi character, played by Ben Stiller, says to the priest, "Jews want their rabbi to be everything they are not." He meant by this that the rabbi is expected to be without blemish, the "symbolic exemplar" of piety and perfection. Unfortunately, for both rabbi and congregation, this collusion of perfectionism harms everyone. The synagogue becomes a community of covering up one's brokenness and imperfection, "looking good" for one another and for the rabbi instead of the rabbi leading the way to dealing with life's struggles and growing together. This charade prevents true connection with one another, with the rabbi, and with the Divine.

Over the thirty years that I have been seeing families broken by addiction, I have often asked if they ever sought help from their rabbi. Almost all of them are shocked by the question, too ashamed to admit their failure to the rabbi: "I'm afraid he would think less of me." I get the same response from the rabbis who struggle with their own addictions. They too feel they have to hide in shame until they are no longer able to cover up their misdeeds and are publicly exposed and humiliated.

It seems to me that too many of us are missing the basic tenets of Judaism. All humans are imperfect by divine design; we are endowed with free will and challenged to choose between opposing inclinations, *yetzer ha-tov* and *yetzer ha-ra*. Both come from God and both are necessary to human existence. God has gifted us with *teshuvah*, the way to repair our souls when we have been seduced by *yetzer ha-ra* and are mired in shame.

Adam and Eve blew it. They disobeyed, enticed by the forbidden, and ate the fruit from the Tree of Knowledge of Good and Bad. I think God knew they would. That was not their sin. Their sin was hiding from God in shame and blaming one another instead of coming clean, admitting their faults, and making *teshuvah*.

These demons known as Shame and Blame have been passed down to us from generation to generation. It's time to rewrite the story. We are all blemished. Instead of covering up our imperfections, misdeeds, and vulnerabilities we have to own and befriend them. We have to live *teshuvah* by admitting our imperfections and misdeeds, making amends to those we have harmed, and making a plan not to repeat them. This is the heart of Jewish living and the essence of Alcoholics Anonymous. Without *teshuvah*, Shame and Blame thrive.

Rabbi Paul Steinberg has written his way out of shame and into recovery through integrating his Jewish learning with the spiritual message of Alcoholics Anonymous. He has done this while living in rehab, "hitting bottom" with a thud. In surrendering his image, title, and awards he has gained humility, integrity, and wholeness (*shalem*), which is the unification of his conflicting inclinations. For much of his life, Rabbi Steinberg was at war with himself. He lived a double life: learned, scholarly, charismatic, honored rabbi in public; shameful, secret drunk and liar in private. His alcoholism and disruptive behavior grew with his success, compelling him to destroy the image he had so carefully constructed. AA lore would say: "God did for him what he couldn't do for himself"—toppled his false self so he could find *wholeness*, unifying the inner and outer selves. The equivalent Jewish teaching is that the good inclination is good and the evil inclination is *very* good.

It is a spiritual and psychological truth that the "brighter the light, the darker the shadow." They grow at the same pace. Therefore, even when the perceived false self—the Image Self—is publicly acclaimed, the shameful, undeserving self shatters the false self in the service of wholeness. Then light can shine through the shattered chaos. That is why the evil inclination is *very* good and why Judaism teaches that in the place where a *Baal Teshuvah* (the person turning to God in repentance) stands, not even the most saintly can reach.

Rabbi Paul Steinberg, in my eyes, is the symbolic exemplar of a *Baal Teshuvah*. He has been to the bottom, publicly exposed, and privately shamed. He has "come out of the closet" from hypocrisy, from saying one thing and doing another. Instead of "preaching," he practices recovering Judaism. He walks his talk; what is in his heart is on his lips. Every day he struggles to take right action when he has wrong thoughts and desires. When he makes a wrong choice, he makes *teshuvah*. This is what builds spiritual muscle.

So I believe that Paul Steinberg is more qualified as rabbi today than he was before his "fall." The role of rabbi ought to be to teach us how to wrestle with God and self, admit mistakes, and make *teshuvah*. Tragically, our culture tells us to maintain appearances at all costs and to "do as I say, not as I do." Rabbi Steinberg's courage to come out of hiding is heroic.

My hope for this book is that it gives people permission to come out of hiding, admit their shameful secrets, and ask for help before they hit bottom. The antidote to addiction is truth. It is time to smash the Idol of Perfection and tell the truth of our human brokenness both within our families and from our pulpits.

—Harriet Rossetto

Introduction

I am a Jew! Hath a Jew not eyes? Hath not a Jew hands,
organs, dimensions, senses, affections, passions? Fed with
the same food, hurt with the same weapons, subject to the
same diseases, healed by the same means, warmed and
cooled by the same winter and summer as a Christian is?
—"Shylock," Shakespeare's *Merchant of Venice*, Act 3, Scene 1

*H*ello, my name is Paul and I'm an alcoholic. This is the hardest
sentence I have ever said aloud. It took me years to be able to
say it and actually mean what I said. After all, alcoholism is a disease
of denial, deceit, and dishonesty, and the alcoholic is masterful at
deceiving the self. Once I started saying it, I also found that my Jewish
identity provided an additional challenge to identifying as an alcoholic.
Whether it was good old-fashioned Jewish guilt, or the unspoken rule
that Jews shouldn't hang our dirty laundry out to dry lest we give anyone an excuse to dislike us, or that being an alcoholic just isn't something that happens to a "nice Jewish boy" (especially a rabbi!), I spent
a long time denying the truth about my disease. After all, what am I
saying about myself when I admit that I'm an alcoholic? Am I a bad
Jew or, worse, a bad person with tainted moral fiber? Am I a failure in
life? Am I intellectually and emotionally inferior to others? Being an
alcoholic carries with it a stigma—a scarlet letter, if you will—in our

society. Adding the weight of the Jewish community's expectations and judgments, my fear was that, with my admission to being an alcoholic, I would forever be doomed to dwell on the margins of society and be rejected by my own Jewish community.

What I discovered in rehab centers and in the rooms of Alcoholics Anonymous, however, was that I was by no means alone. Not only are there tens of millions of alcoholics in the United States, but a substantial number of them are Jews. I also learned that alcoholics and drug addicts are not bad people at all; they are not bad people trying to be good, but rather sick people trying to get healthy. It is true that in the throes of the disease, alcoholics will make odd, destructive, and even shocking choices at the expense of relationships, financial stability, jobs, and life itself. This contributes to the stigma and confusion about the nature of alcoholism and our understanding of it as a legitimate disease. It is certainly a disease and precisely because of the insane choices and behavior that accompanies it, no one is more confused and frustrated about it than alcoholics themselves.

I also learned, however, that beyond the suffering and mental slavery to which alcoholism subjects the alcoholic, there is a life of freedom—spiritual freedom—that awaits the eventually sober man or woman. The remedy to this disease is a spiritual one that involves mind, body, and heart. It can be learned through the wisdom of Judaism that for thousands and thousands of years has worked as a wise and good approach to life for millions and millions of people. There is also wisdom and guidance to be found in the Steps of Alcoholics Anonymous (AA). These AA Steps, found in the *Big Book* and *12 and 12* (*Twelve Steps and Twelve Traditions*) of Alcoholics Anonymous comprise spiritual principles transmitted through loving and tireless sponsors who themselves have had the power to crawl out of the disease's incomprehensible demoralization. And they were only able to do so because of the grace of the sponsor who had earlier refused to disregard them as invisible, a lost cause, or a pariah. The spiritual lessons of individual and communal experience, hope, and strength found in both Judaism and AA save countless lives, as they are passed on from one person to the next. So this solution to the disease of alcoholism is passed down from generation to generation—*le'dor va-dor*.

Because the nature of the remedy and the solution is spiritual, we can see clear parallels between Judaism and the AA approach. Unfortunately, many Jews may either be unable to grasp the inherent parallels to their own Judaism or choose to entirely dismiss Judaism (and organized religion) altogether because it has not "worked" thus far. This book is a response to that very issue, bringing Judaism from the margins of our recovery right into the black print of the *Big Book* itself. The premise of this work is that Judaism, through its values and practices, can serve as a spiritual remedy to alcoholism, as well as enrich and expand AA principles, adding more depth, more meaning, and more tools for recovery. Of course, not every word in the *Big Book* may align with every Jewish concept, as both are subject to interpretation. However, there are certainly enough parallels to discern a kinship between the two.

Therefore, my purpose here is not to write about AA or how to do AA. That is something that each of us must learn with our sponsor. I intend to merely glean insights from the helpful concepts of AA as I learned them with my sponsor, counselors, and many anonymous sages who passed through meetings in church basements and fellowship halls. In the end, this is a book about Judaism as a resource and building block for recovery. As a rabbi and Jewish educator, I found myself continually referencing my Jewish spirituality throughout my recovery. At times, I found that Judaism enriched AA and even improved on it. Consequently, what I share here is gathered from notes I made in the margins of my *Big Book* and my hope is to humbly share what helps me to deepen and enrich both my sobriety and my Jewish spirituality. And, truth be told, putting this book together helps me in the progress of my own recovery. I hope to draw from the margins to build a bridge back to the center, to the heart and core of life.

Part I

A Judaism of Experience, Strength, and Hope

A Rabbi's Journey through Alcoholism

> More than most people I think alcoholics want to know who they are, what life is all about, whether they have a divine origin and an appointed destiny, live in a system of cosmic justice and love.
>
> —Bill Wilson, *The AA Way of Life*

Like many alcoholics, I have never felt comfortable in my own skin. As far back as I can remember, I felt like an outsider and disconnected from the center of social groups, including my own family. I desperately wanted to be liked and accepted, and I found myself competing to be affirmed by being the best at sports, which was an arena in which I found early success. And even though I was naturally good at athletics, my own successes surprised me; through my distorted lens, I struggled to accept that I was truly good at anything. When it came to my studies, I didn't quite see the point and essentially checked out of most of my classes until the very end of high school, when I excelled.

I was fortunate enough to have a very tight-knit group of friends in high school and we did everything together, including going to weekend parties. At these parties, beer flowed from the taps, and my mission was to simply get as much of it in me as possible. Girls were very important to me, but if talking to any of them was called for, I would focus my attention on the one sure thing—alcohol. When that bitter, frothy potion went down and burned my stomach, my mind suddenly stopped racing. I was relieved of my concern that I wasn't good-looking enough, smart enough, likable enough, and I didn't have to obsess anymore. All I had to do was keep drinking. By seventeen, I knew exactly what I liked doing, and weekend parties could not come fast enough.

Then I went to college because that was what I was supposed to do, not because I especially wanted to go. College provided me with new drinking and "partying" connections. There the weekend party seemed to start on Thursday nights and often extended late into Monday nights. Moreover, my new friends knew how to get marijuana, cocaine, ecstasy, and everything under the sun. I had no idea what any of them were, but with alcohol on my breath, I was game for them all.

Eventually, my college courses got in the way of my drinking and using, so I stopped going. I still managed, however, to play basketball and exercise, so my youthful appearance remained, which probably served as a good cover for my behavior. However, the day came when I would have to admit to my parents (who were funding my college education) that I had secretly withdrawn from my courses and I was no longer enrolled. Of course, I had yet to realize that this had anything to do with my drinking and using.

My parents, who had recently been reinspired by their Judaism, thought that sending me to a kibbutz in Israel would be a good idea.

And it was. On the kibbutz, I learned hard work and discipline, and discovered a contentment that I had not found in the classroom. Yet, my drinking and using continued unabated. Because beer was expensive on the kibbutz, I learned to appreciate vodka as an easier path to where I wanted to go (especially under the tutelage of my Russian brothers and sisters who were doing the Hebrew language *ulpan* as part of their recent immigration, or *aliyah*).

After nearly a year, I returned home from Israel with a newfound appreciation for my Jewish identity and a thirst to learn more about it. I kept drinking and using, as I realized that I could be quite functional in society, even with my "partying." I got a job, met a great girl, and soon completed my degree. My girlfriend and I then decided that I should continue my educational path, particularly in something Jewish, since I had a newfound passion for it. I applied to a dozen religious and Jewish studies graduate programs, yet was turned down by them all; my academic career was the only concrete evidence of my destructive path.

As luck would have it, the graduate school of education at American Jewish University (AJU), which trained Jewish educators, gave me a chance under the condition of probation. Now, however, I was living with my girlfriend and my alcoholic life was reduced to beer and wine only on weekends. Because of my genuine interest in the field, academic success came easily. Professors in the rabbinical school adjoining AJU took notice of my potential and I was invited to apply; after all, as one professor pointed out, a rabbi is really a Jewish educator, and that's what I was good at. Although the thought of becoming a rabbi was a bit bizarre to me, I did not have any better ideas.

My girlfriend and I then married, and she began to talk about my drinking being a problem. Being an alcoholic seemed as though it was for outcasts only—people with *real problems*, not me. Sure, I had addiction in my family, but that wasn't me—it couldn't be me. Still, I promised to cut back. This is when I started to lie. My lying increased when we had our first child and I was secretly drinking on weeknights in addition to consuming wine and beer on weekends.

After my rabbinic ordination, we moved to Dallas, and again I restricted my drinking to weekends only. As time went on, however, the progressive nature of the disease kicked in and my drinking increased again. Another child arrived in our growing family and my career was showing continuing signs of success. The obsession with alcohol was now entrenched in my mind and I used all my creative acumen to drink as often as possible. I sought out whatever had as little scent as possible, perhaps hard lemonade or vodka. My wife steadily grew more frustrated and despairing. Our fights led to sincere apologies, vows, and then the ritual making up. Even though the apologies and promises to stop were sincere, like the sirens calling out to Odysseus, the horrifying, beastly voice of selfishness and self-deception consistently found justification in another trip to the liquor store.

Luckily, I was a functional alcoholic, managing to always produce quality results in my work, and soon I was called to a bigger job in Los Angeles. This time, my drinking was constant and, even though drinking almost always led to misery, I could not and would not stop. My wife and I had begun to use the word *alcoholic*, but I never truly identified as one in my heart.

This was followed by another four years of lying—lying to my employer and colleagues, and lying to my wife and family about what I was really doing. I fell down into the inferno of perpetual shame and, despite my own suffering, despite the fact that I knew my suffering was caused by alcohol, I could not stop. There were days I would take my first drink with tears in my eyes, knowing what was about to happen. Finally, after my wife issued an ultimatum, I humbled myself enough to enter my first rehabilitation center. Although the rehab led to some early success, it was followed by a series of relapses. After a harrowing few months, I found myself in and out of rehabilitation centers, experiencing completely pitiful and incomprehensible demoralization. By the grace and compassion of my friend Rabbi Mark Borowitz, I entered Beit T'Shuvah in Los

Angeles, a Jewish rehabilitation and spiritual center, where Mark is the chief operating officer.

Some may wonder how a rabbi, a man who acquired several advanced degrees and communal (and, in my case, national) prestige, could reconcile his alcoholism. Some may further ask how a "man of God and Torah" could live with himself in such a condition. There were many times I asked myself the same thing. I seriously wondered whether I might do everyone a favor if I relieved the planet of my existence. I did not want to suffer like this, I did not want to hurt my wife and my kids, or disappoint my community, or lose everything for which I had worked so hard. Who plans for such a life? Yet, my urge was to drink, as a way to feel any sort of relief, and I couldn't stop. If it were not for my children, I wonder if I would have survived.

I acknowledge that there may be stunned friends and colleagues reading this account. But these words are not specifically meant for them; they are for the suffering alcoholics in their midst. I am writing in hopes that my story will resonate with them and that shared hope and strength may emerge. We are brothers and sisters in arms and the Jewish alcoholic may be as confounded as I have been in finding a pathway back to a spiritual and Jewish identity. We alcoholics have the opportunity to make *teshuvah*, a return to a peaceful, spiritual core—to our genuine, integrated selves—when we can identify our shared problem together and then choose to shift our perspective toward the joy and fulfillment that life offers us without alcohol.

The solution is rooted in what AA founder Bill Wilson says in his own story: "Simple, but not easy; a price had to be paid. It meant destruction of self-centeredness. I must turn in all things to the Father of Light who presides over all."[1] Or, as the great Jewish thinker Abraham Joshua Heschel wrote: "New insight begins when satisfaction comes to an end, when all that has been seen, said, or done looks like a distortion.... Man's true fulfillment depends on communion with that which transcends him."[2]

Chapter 1

Understanding Addiction, Jewish Spirituality, and Medicine

> There is evolution but we human beings are a crucial part of evolution. Torah is the conscience that helps direct the arc of nature's trajectory. Judaism and science are not in opposition, but allies in *tikkun olam*—the repair of the world that cries out for human intervention for godly purpose.
>
> —Rabbi Harold M. Schulweis, "Secular Science and Jewish Faith"

Judaism is a spiritual approach to being a human being in the world. It is also a mature spiritual approach by virtue of the fact that it does not close itself off to outside disciplines of knowledge and wisdom. This maturity may be precisely what Ben Zoma, a second-century sage, meant when he said: "Who is wise? One who learns from all men."[1]

There are some Jews today who resist all disciplines of knowledge outside the Jewish world, and this is very unfortunate. It should be noted, however, that since the dawn of Judaism, Jewish sages and leaders have integrated and incorporated outside disciplines of knowledge into Jewish traditions and ideology. One may strongly argue that this integration allowed Judaism to evolve and, frankly, survive during the millennia of Diaspora. Many revered rabbis who greatly influenced the Jewish tradition were themselves well educated outside the Jewish tradition, including physicians, astronomers, and philosophers (i.e., scientists of their day). Thus, Judaism as a spiritual approach is not antithetical or hostile to the schools of contemporary science.

Addiction and Choice

Even though addiction is a spiritual malady, we can unhesitatingly affirm that it is also rooted in biology. Understanding addiction as a genetically influenced disease (60 percent genetic, 40 percent environmental)[2] centered in the brain provides us with yet more tools and leverage to achieve healing and wholeness. Moreover, understanding the brain science of addiction removes the moral stigma associated with it, as we learn that drinking and using are not merely the result of a "bad person" making a "bad choice." Addiction is a physiological response. Therefore, combining spiritual and medical treatment may offer a powerful antidote to the disease.

So, what is addiction? There are several competing theories about addiction, yet the strongest medical perspective contends that it is a disease with the brain as its target organ. There are many symptoms, including (1) biological symptoms, such as liver disease, high blood pressure, and nerve damage; (2) social and emotional symptoms, such as depression, anxiety, poor performance, divorce, and legal problems; and (3) spiritual symptoms, such as hopelessness, alienation, and debilitating shame.

The part of the brain most affected by addiction is the midbrain (or the reptilian brain), which is primarily responsible for our survival behaviors, such as fleeing from danger, eating and digestion, breathing, and procreation. Survival behaviors are reinforced in our system by the sensation of "feeling good." In other words, the things that feel good, taste good, and give us pleasure are all related to survival.

For example, many of us like the taste of chocolate cake. Chocolate cake contains a lot carbohydrates, sugar, and fat. Those ingredients are all great for survival, especially during a drought or famine; the calories from carbohydrates, sugar, and fat can sustain us for a long time. On the other hand, some of us do not care for the taste of broccoli, at least not as much as the taste of chocolate cake. Broccoli certainly has wonderful nutrients that keep us healthy, but broccoli's nutritional benefits are short-lived because it has so few calories and will not last during a drought or famine; we could not survive on broccoli alone, whereas we might by eating nothing but chocolate cake. In this case, the brain evolved so that it rewards us with a pleasing taste for the food that is best for survival.[3]

The good feeling we experience from these survival behaviors stems from the brain releasing dopamine, a neurotransmitter that gives us a sense of euphoria. The problem with drinking and using is that they cause between two and ten times more dopamine to flood into the system than natural rewards do. The "high" from drinking and using is bigger and longer lasting than the one from eating chocolate cake. Over time and with repeated use, the brain compensates for this huge high from drinking and using by lowering the natural amount of dopamine produced by the brain. As a result, alcoholics and addicts need to drink and use more and more often, not only to get high but also to merely sustain normal levels of dopamine. Moreover, the brain has now become accustomed to the use of alcohol and drugs, and rewards alcohol and drug use as a survival behavior, so it actually trumps other survival behaviors, including eating and sleeping.

Now we can understand the phenomenon of craving. Alcoholics and addicts do not crave their substance in a superficial manner. It is not like the craving for something sweet after a good meal. A craving is caused by the brain seeking to produce higher levels of dopamine to ensure our survival. In other words, the brain is sending messages that it needs more dopamine as a basic requirement for survival. Therefore, alcoholics or addicts experience a strong sense of urgency and anxiety, and feel as though they must absolutely get their drink or drug as soon as possible or they will "jump out of their skin." Cravings are actually a form of physical suffering.

Treating Body and Soul

Therapy may vary for each alcoholic and addict, especially if we have a dual diagnosis. A dual diagnosis means that we are diagnosed as an alcoholic or addict, in addition to another social or emotional disorder, including attention deficit disorder (ADD), attention deficit/hyperactivity disorder (ADHD), or bipolar disorder. That being said, the basic therapy will help balance the dopamine levels in the brain. This can be accomplished with medication. But medication alone is simply not enough. We must also practice healthy lifestyle habits that reinforce the natural rewards of the brain. Our brain literally needs to change by shutting down the previous neural pathways that it has been accustomed to and forging different, healthier routes. The brain will change as our experience changes, by behaving differently and responding to our life and impulses differently. This requires us to change our old habits and adopt healthy new behaviors, replacing our old lifestyle and destructive habits with positive and life-affirming ones.

These habits should address the whole human experience—mind, body, and soul. Judaism holds that mind, body, and soul are interrelated, with each affecting the other.[4] Perhaps the greatest proponent of this idea was Maimonides (1135–1204, Spain and Egypt). In his code of laws, the Mishneh Torah, Maimonides, a physician by trade, argues that we need proper balance in our life. He contends that physical exercise and balanced eating help clear and focus the mind, and ultimately enable us to behave properly in accordance with our spiritual principles.[5] Such habits are cultivated and learned through repetition. Recovery, therefore, is a process of learning, educating the mind, body, and soul to live a good life to our fullest potential. It takes a lot of work and often requires significant life changes that take time, as the brain, body, mind, and soul all begin to work in natural, integrated harmony instead of in conflict. Once the initial changes take place, maintenance through spiritual practice and, in some cases, continued medication is necessary for lifelong recovery.

Personal Reflections

At first, drinking and using was fun. In high school and college, alcohol and drugs were a means of letting loose and having a "wild time." I could go to a club and dance freely, I could make outrageous jokes with buddies, and I could flirt with girls with little anxiety. At the time, I did not think about whether or not I was addicted or whether it was right or wrong. It was just what I did and what a lot of other people did.

As I got older, got married, had kids, and got a job, drinking and everything that came with it changed. Within the course of a couple of years, those activities that characterized my social life and gave me a sense of release and fun were now inappropriate and unavailable. All of a sudden, it seemed as if my youth was gone and the weight of responsibility and adulthood was all-encompassing.

I remember drinking beer and wine as an end-of-the-week "treat," a reward for suffering through the weekly, mundane pains of adulthood. Looking back now, I realize that I didn't have healthy activities and fun that gave me balance. Or maybe I didn't allow myself to have any of those activities because they were expensive and I didn't think I was worth it.

There came a point in my drinking when it was the only way I knew how to let go. I had to drink or I was uncomfortable. I resented situations or people that kept me from my drink. Then the pain deepened because I felt guilty for even having those feelings of discomfort and resentment—why, after all, should I feel discomfort and how can I resent something and get angry just because I was kept from drinking? How could I have these horrible thoughts and feelings all in the name of getting loaded? And then, once I did take that drink, after the initial high, I felt ashamed again—all this confusion and trouble just for this? All this just to be alone with the bottle?

Today, I take comfort in knowing that the mountain of addiction is spiritual as well as biological. I am comforted to know that it was so hard to stop because I was fighting not only my spiritual "demons" but also the very chemistry of my brain. And I am comforted by the hope that comes from knowing better what the problem is so I can better address and fix it. I now know that if I change my brain chemistry by changing my habits and thinking, and I can live a sober, healthy life.

Chapter 2

A God and Religion of Recovery

If a person says to you, I have labored and not found, do not believe him. If he says, I have not labored, but still have found, do not believe him. If he says, I have labored and found—believe him. (B. Talmud, *Megillah* 6b)

Discovering God

One of the most precious gifts that both Judaism and AA offer those of us in recovery is the intellectual opportunity to believe freely. We are invited to develop our own spirituality. While both Judaism and AA emphasize that belief is extremely important, what we believe, "God as we understood Him," is left open for each of us to discover on our own.

The resistance to precisely defining God in both Judaism and AA is very wise. No one can truly transmit a spiritual awakening to someone else; we can only model its results and speak about it. Spirituality

13

itself is primarily learned by personal experience and by relating our personal stories to those of others and the world around us. And, as the appendix in the *Big Book*, called "The Spiritual Experience," points out, hardly any of us experience a radical, transcendent event of spiritual awakening that changes everything in our lives. Rarely does someone have that "aha" moment. Instead, it says:

> Most of our experiences are what the psychologist William James calls the "educational variety" because they develop slowly over a period of time. Quite often friends of the new-comer are aware of the difference long before he is himself. He finally realizes that he has undergone a profound alteration in his reaction to life; that such a change could hardly have been brought about by himself alone.[1]

Therefore, spirituality begins from a very personal and individual place. We must admit that we encounter God from where we uniquely stand in the world; no one else stands where we stand. "Standing," however, is merely a metaphor for identifying our spiritual locale at any given moment. Spiritually speaking, none of us actually "stands" in one place, because we never remain in spiritual stasis. With each thought, each feeling, and each action, our spiritual location moves. We are dynamic beings, always in flux, which only adds to the unique manner of our own distinct connection with the Divine.

A God That Is Mine and Ours

The sages of the Jewish tradition make it clear that each of us has our own unique relationship with God. But they also are clear that our spirituality cannot and should not exist in a vacuum. We are exposed to both historical and contemporary spiritual ideas. Judaism has thrived for thousands of years before our arrival on earth, and we are wise to pay careful attention to what has worked for those who came before us. The sages derive this stance by interpreting the opening line of the central Jewish prayer, the *Amidah* (i.e., the "standing" prayer). The prayer begins:

> Blessed are You, God, our God, God of Abraham, God of Isaac, and God of Jacob [some add: God of Sarah, God of Rebekkah, God of Leah, and God of Rachel].

At first glance, the rabbis point out this opening blessing is problematic because it appears redundant. After all, why does the phrase *God of* have to precede the name of each patriarch (and matriarch)? In other words, why can't it simply say, "God of Abraham, Isaac, and Jacob"? Why the seemingly superfluous phrasing?

The rabbis go on to explain that, although each of the ancestors connected and had a relationship with God, even the same God, each of them related to the Divine in their own unique way.[2] They may have formed their conception and relationship with God based on how their parents understood God, but they still developed their own. In his book, *Ten Rungs*, the Jewish philosopher Martin Buber sums up this interpretation:

> There are two kinds of people who believe in God. One believes because he has taken over the faith of his fathers, and his faith is strong. The other has arrived at faith through thinking and studying. The difference between them is this: The advantage of the first is that, no matter what arguments may be brought against it, his faith cannot be shaken; his faith is firm because it was taken from his fathers. But there is one flaw in it: He has faith only in response to the command of man, and he has acquired it without studying and thinking for himself. The advantage of the second is that, because he found God through much thinking, he has arrived at a faith of his own.

But here too there is a flaw: it is easy to shake his faith by refuting it through evidence. But he who unites both kinds of faith is invincible....

The same interpretation has been given to our saying, "God of Abraham, God of Isaac, God of Jacob," and not "God of Abraham, Isaac, and Jacob," for this indicates that Isaac and Jacob did not merely take over the tradition of Abraham; they themselves searched for God.[3]

Drawing from this teaching, we can learn three important lessons about faith and belief. One is that we should neither dismiss nor disparage our ancestors' conceptions of God. Instead, we can learn from them. While we may not always accept their ideas or beliefs, we should not cast them aside either, showing contempt prior to investigation. We should use their spiritual searching and connection to strengthen our own spiritual searching and connection—their experience informs our experience. Also, there is a great spiritual benefit to seeing ourself as a part of an ongoing spiritual evolution through the chain of history.

The second lesson is that Judaism, as a spiritual approach, makes room for doubt. Doubt is not the opposite of faith. The opposite of faith is either complacency, which is blowing off the question of God, or hubris, which is acting as if we have it all figured out. The opposite of faith is, therefore, not having the courage to remain open-minded, and to continually ask life's most important questions. Doubt, on the other hand, provides the personal texture and fabric that weaves through our beliefs, and ultimately keeps us grounded and humble.

Third, we learn that we need to cultivate our own understanding of and relationship with God—a God as we, each one of us, understands the Divine. Simply put, there is no one Jewish way to believe in God. The only dogma is that God can never be a human being and that there is but one God alone. But that does not let us off the hook in terms of doing our own work to connect with God. Rather, with our intellectual and spiritual freedom comes the responsibility to do our own spiritual digging, by learning and reflecting on our own experiences as they relate to spiritual ideas and practices. When there is no single answer or path, we must rigorously construct our own, using the inroads already available to us, as well as paving our own when we must.

The Dynamic Relationship

As we forge our relationship with God, we first discover that we have not yet found God. We are on the road. We are walking toward God, moving closer with each moment. We are dynamic, changing beings. And as we get closer and our relationship with God becomes stronger, we learn that, like us, God is also dynamic, moving, and changing. When Moses encounters God at the burning bush (Exod. 3:14) and he asks God for God's name, God replies, *Ehyeh asher Ehyeh*, literally, "I will be what I will be." It is not a name that is in the present tense, as it is often mistranslated. It is in the future tense, denoting the constant, unfixed, continuously creating, and continuously becoming of God and the universe. Our spiritual goal in relating with God is to see our changing dynamism in concert with God's changing dynamism. In Rabban Gamliel's words: "To do God's will as though it were yours, and that God will do your will as though it were God's."[4] Again, we turn to Martin Buber, who provides a beautiful description of the dynamic experience of Jewish spirituality:

> The world is a spinning die, and everything turns and changes: Man is turned into angel, and angel into man, and head into foot, and the foot into the head. Thus all things turn and spin and change, this into that, and that into this, the topmost to the undermost, and the undermost to the topmost. For at the root all is one.[5]

Discovering Religion

If faith and belief are open and undefined, whereby each of us is entitled to think about, doubt, and relate to God differently, what, then, is religion? The term *religion*, by the way, is not an originally Jewish term or idea. In fact, the Hebrew word for *religion* (*dat*) largely came into use only in the early twentieth century, when modern Hebrew began to be spoken in Israel. Until then, Jews predominantly referred to their religious identity as being part of a nation of people who lived by the Torah.

Today, especially in the Western world, *religion* is often understood as a set of our personal beliefs in God; it is a synonym for *faith*. That is not Judaism. Faith and how we may express our faith in God are parts of Judaism, but not nearly all of it. When we say Judaism is a religion, we mean something altogether different.

First, Judaism is a religion in the sense that it is based on the claim that life is infinitely meaningful and spiritual. Each of us is made of both stardust and the divine sparks of infinity. Everything we do is meaningful and we are bound together, each of us as ripples in the sea of God's infinity of energy and love. This spirituality is not Jewish; God is not a Jew. I may be a Jew. We may be Jews. Our communities may be Jewish communities, yet everything we do is shaped by and reflects that we are human beings on this planet in relationship with a God that is as vast and as infinite as the cosmos. There are many paths to God in our human experience and all paths are divinely chosen in their own way. Thankfully, Judaism is a deeply wise one.

Another way Judaism could be understood as a religion is in the way that the twelfth-century scholar Maimonides described it. In his *Guide of the Perplexed*,[6] he essentially defines religion when he argues on behalf of two religious endeavors: *tikkun ha-nefesh* and *tikkun ha-guf*—fixing the soul and fixing the body. And by fixing the body, he meant fixing the world. So Judaism invites us to inculcate deep thinking, inculcate a deep spiritual and emotional openness, and engage in activities and rituals that foster personal meaning. Jews are also asked to see to it that the realm of the body, the world here and now, is healthy, meaning that we have an obligation to feed each other, clothe each other, and take care of each other and the planet. *Tikkun ha-nefesh* seeks to make people better people and *tikkun ha-guf* seeks to make the world a better world. If an effort is not designed to both heal the self and heal the world, Judaism is simply not interested.

Judaism may, therefore, be understood as a religion in the etymological sense of the word. The English word *religion* comes from the root *lig*, meaning "to connect." Hasidism discovered this understanding of Judaism when it linked the Aramaic word for connection, *tzavta*, with the Hebrew word for performing a Jewish practice or ritual, *mitzvah*. Hasidim explained that since the words share nearly the same letters and sounds, we learn that performing a religious act is a form of connection. In short, Judaism seeks to connect us with God, with others, and with ourself.

Beyond Faith and Reason

Judaism is further distinguished as a religion because it is characterized as both a faithful and a rational path.[7] What is faithful? *Faithful* means trusting that the path is a real path. Franz Rosenzweig, the great early-twentieth-century Jewish thinker, writes about this when discussing the idea of verification. He asks, How can we prove a religious point? Only in the fact, he says, that people have staked their lives upon it.[8] Judaism is a religious path on which millions and millions of people over thousands of years have staked their lives. Amid the world's desert and wilderness, Judaism has provided deep wells of wisdom and hope, and invigorating aquifers of holiness and beauty.

Faithful means that our spirituality goes beyond ourself and puts that spirituality into action, as we make behavioral commitments for our own sake and for the sake of others. We are faithful that our Jewish practices and rituals, the *mitzvot*, which are communally imbued and entrusted to the Jewish people, help us in practically all areas of life. They inform how we govern, how we worship, how we eat, how we feed other people, how we work, how we rest, how we love, and how we buy, sell, and borrow. Judaism as a religion trusts that these deeds are inherently wise and will sanctify our lives, making each of us a better person and the world a better place. We may not always observe the *mitzvot* as thoroughly as we might, but we are open to their wisdom and leave room for the possibility of further observance.

And Judaism is a rational religion. It is *rational* because it requires that, even when we are faithful and even when we accept the tradition and the *mitzvot* as they have come down to us, we have to be reasonable and sane. That is, reasonable and sane enough to think critically and recognize the path's fallibility. If we are not self-critical enough to recognize the bad religious decisions that the Jewish tradition has made over time, then we are small-minded and dishonest. This means that, at times, after careful study, we may find that the *mitzvot* and customs of the past should not be kept in our time because they offend what we have discovered to be ethical (e.g., the equality of women, gays, and lesbians). We are supposed to be faithful enough to see that the path is wise and holy and also *rational* enough to see that it is imperfect and can still be further sanctified. In this way, Judaism makes space for us to continually grow in our spirituality and make it our own.

Judaism is not always easy because it demands a certain behavioral standard. It is also not easy because it expects us to engage our intellects. That said, the practices and the study that they encourage teach us that life is not to be taken for granted. It is constantly cheering us on to be better and to fulfill our potential. It allows us to think freely because God has faith in us, and it asks us to behave in a proper manner to show our faith in God. In short, life matters and we matter.

Personal Reflections

When I was twenty-one years old, I found myself smoking pot every day and drinking a lot, too. My girlfriend of three years—whom I loved—broke up with me and moved on to work in a strip club. I had also dropped out of college without telling my parents about it.

I just didn't see the point of attending classes. Why go to classes? They're boring and the homework is annoying. Why should I get a degree? For what—to get a job? So then what? So I can make money and get a house, a car, get married, and have kids? I saw a lot of people doing all those things and they were still miserable. They call it a midlife crisis. Plus, don't we all just die anyway? And it doesn't really matter whether anyone is good or bad, a thief or a philanthropist, a junkie or a guru. We all die to nothingness.

I thought a lot about my older brother, an addict who committed suicide in his mid-twenties. Why shouldn't I just kill myself, I thought. It would save a lot of time and I didn't need to go through all the trouble of college and work.

With these questions in mind, I walked out of my apartment into Tucson's baking sun and sat down on the ground to smoke a cigarette and think about suicide options. I looked down and flicked an ash near an anthill. The thought of crushing an ant passed through my mind. I thought, if I kill this ant it won't matter to me. But that ant might be carrying information back to the other ants that they need. Plus, that ant might have a family that needs him or loves him. Killing this ant might actually be the most monumental thing that happens to the anthill. I wondered if I pulled out a blade of grass what impact that might have on the rest of the grass and all the creatures that lived in that ecosystem.

It then occurred to me that even though some things may seem insignificant to some of us, those same things might mean everything to others. Maybe, I realized, just maybe, everything we do has an immeasurable effect on the world. Maybe there really is a "butterfly effect" with everything that exists, every rock we touch, ever ripple of water we make, every action we take. It struck me that things cannot be sort of significant. Either everything is meaningful or nothing is meaningful. Either everything is of God or nothing is. After all, just because something like a leaf or a piece of trash or a dirty look directed at someone may not be meaningful to me, it might be everything to someone else, which then has an impact on everything around that individual.

So, I thought, I have a choice: Either I care about everything I come in contact with or I care about nothing. Either everything I do is meaningful or nothing is. Why did I think that everything could be meaningful? I don't know. Maybe it's my genetics. Maybe it's the way I was raised and that I was indoctrinated to care. Or maybe I have a soul and my soul is connected to everything. I could never know. But, then and there, I realized that I do care about myself and what I do in life. I care and, since I care, I should live life as if I care. I should live a life of meaning and integrity. I will live life as if God is everything and within everything. Thus launched my impulse to change my life, which led to living on an Israeli kibbutz and, ultimately, becoming a rabbi.

Over time, I lost that clarity and that sense of purpose, and I rediscovered drinking. My recovery is strongly connected to recovering my spiritual clarity—that same clarity I had sitting outside in the desert sun, watching ants come and go.

Chapter 3

The Dignity of the Self

Hillel taught: If I am not for myself, who will be? But if am only for myself, what am I? If not now, when? (Mishnah, *Avot* 1:14)

Why, according to the Torah, did God begin creating human beings by only creating one—Adam? It would seem that God could do anything. The first command God gives to humanity is *be fruitful and multiply, fill the earth and master it* (Gen. 1:28), so why go through the trouble of starting with one? Why not a million? Or a hundred? Or even ten? Why begin with one human being from whom the rest of humanity descends?

This is the question that contemporary scholar and author Rabbi Yitz Greenberg frequently asks. His answer is profound and provides an authentic vision of how Judaism understands the self.[1] He utilizes a rabbinic legal source as his proof text. The source, from the Mishnah (c. 200 CE), discusses how the rabbinic court should prepare the witnesses in a capital case, that is, a death penalty case. Obviously, serving as a witness in a capital case carries great weight, since the witnesses are part of the decision as to whether the defendant will be executed and lose his life. The text begins with some typical legal language and then transitions to an explanation of the very question Rabbi Greenberg asks. Why did God start the creation of humanity with one person alone? The Mishnah says:

> Therefore, humans were created singly, to teach you that whoever destroys a single life, Scripture accounts it as if he had destroyed a whole world; and whoever saves one life, Scripture accounts it as if he had saved a whole world. And for the sake of peace among people, that one should not say to his or her fellow, "My father is greater than your father"; and that heretics should not say, "There are many powers in Heaven." Again, to declare the greatness of the Holy One, blessed be God, for a person stamps out many coins with one seal, and they are all alike, but the King, the King of kings, the Holy One, blessed be God, stamps each person with the seal of Adam, and not one of them is like his or her fellow. Therefore each and every one is obligated to say, "For my sake the world was created."[2]

Upon careful study, we see that there are actually three answers as to why God began the creation of humanity with one person. These three answers are what Greenberg calls the three dignities of the human being: (1) the dignity of infinite value; (2) the dignity of equality; and (3) the dignity of uniqueness.

The Dignity of Infinite Value

If you were to ask a parent, "How much is your child worth?" how might that parent respond? Imagine that the buyer would kill the child once purchased; the parent as the seller totally relinquishes any responsibility and connection when the child is sold. How much might the parent sell her child for? $5,000? $50,000? $5 million?

The question is a bit absurd. How can anyone put a price tag on a life? There may be sociopaths who are able to seriously consider that question, but for most of us, it is simply impossible to put a price on a human life. Why is that? Why is it so unthinkable to allow a child to be murdered for money? The Mishnah above answers this question, saying: "Whoever destroys a single life, Scripture [the Torah] accounts it as if he had destroyed a whole world; whoever saves one life, Scripture accounts it as if he had saved a whole world." Simply put, one human life is equivalent to a whole world—that is its value.

But how is a human life like a whole world? For one, a human being, when coupled with another, is able to procreate and generate offspring. So it is that the world began with Adam alone. However, when Adam divided into two and Eve was introduced, the two of them were able to have offspring. Their offspring then had their own offspring, and so on and so forth all the way to us here today. We, like Adam and Eve, have this procreative ability. From one of us alone, many, many more can descend. In this way, we all represent a potential world, and if one of us is destroyed, the potential world of people who would descend from us is destroyed, too. We may be reminded of the finale of the film *Schindler's List,* the story of Oskar Schindler and the hundreds of Jews he saved from perishing in the Holocaust. The finale shows the children and grandchildren of those Schindler saved—the worlds he had saved—while the quotation from this Mishnah appears: "Whoever saves one life, Scripture accounts it as if he had saved a whole world."

That interpretation, however, seems insufficient because we all realize that our potential as "a world unto ourselves" is far beyond our mere physical, procreative powers. Each of us also has an internal world. And our internal world—our feelings, our thoughts, our love, and our energy—is much more profound than our external one, as it has tremendous influence beyond parenthood. Using the case of selling a child again, if the parent were to sell that child and allow him to be destroyed, the parent would be doing so having no idea what that child could become. That child could become the next president of the United States. He could become a scientist and cure the world's most deadly diseases. He could be the next great rabbi, whose writings are studied and quoted by generations of future scholars. He could become a teacher who inspires countless others to achieve their potential. He could be one of a billion types of people who could have an infinite circle of influence that extends even beyond his own lifetime. After all, the rabbinic sages proclaim that our good deeds are akin to our offspring because they live on through others.[3]

Therefore, according to Judaism, the first dignity of being human is that each of us has infinite potential in the world. For whatever reason, maybe because of messages we get from the media and the greater society, or maybe because of childhood traumas, or because of the lies we tell ourselves, we sadly forget or deny this about our lives. Many of us are more inclined to believe that we are worthless, rather than opening our eyes to ways in which we touch and influence others and the world around us every day. When we lose sight of our infinite worth, the worlds that emanate from us, it becomes much easier for us to throw up our hands and protest that everything is utter futility. "Why shouldn't I drink or use?" "What does it matter—nothing ever changes?" "Nobody really cares anyway." Such voices, which we all hear at one point or another, become much more convincing when we fail to acknowledge the infinite potential of our soul.

Consider the most expensive painting in the world. As of now, the most expensive painting in the world is Paul Cézanne's *The Card Players*, which was auctioned for an estimated $269 million. Now, imagine that once the buyer bought that painting, he arrived at his porch and was just too tired and too frustrated to carry it up to his penthouse. "What's the point, anyway?" he said to himself. "I'll get it in the morning." So he just left it in the street where it could be kicked, spat upon, or stolen. Insane, right? No one would ever do that. If you bought a $269 million painting, you would treat it ... well, like a $269 million painting. You would take every precaution to treat it

Fill in this card and return it to us to be eligible for our quarterly drawing for a $100 gift certificate for Jewish Lights books.

We hope that you will enjoy this book and find it useful in enriching your life.

Book title: _____

Your comments: _____

How you learned of this book: _____

If purchased: Bookseller _____ City _____ State _____

Please send me a free JEWISH LIGHTS Publishing catalog. I am interested in: (check all that apply)

1. ☐ Spirituality
2. ☐ Mysticism/Kabbalah
3. ☐ Philosophy/Theology
4. ☐ History/Politics

5. ☐ Women's Interest
6. ☐ Environmental Interest
7. ☐ Healing/Recovery
8. ☐ Children's Books

9. ☐ Caregiving/Grieving
10. ☐ Ideas for Book Groups
11. ☐ Religious Education Resources
12. ☐ Interfaith Resources

Name (PRINT) _____

Street _____

City _____ State _____ Zip _____

E-MAIL (FOR SPECIAL OFFERS ONLY) _____

Please send a JEWISH LIGHTS Publishing catalog to my friend:

Name (PRINT) _____

Street _____

City _____ State _____ Zip _____

JEWISH LIGHTS PUBLISHING
Tel: (802) 457-4000 • Fax: (802) 457-4004
Available at better booksellers. Visit us online at www.jewishlights.com

gently, care for it, and preserve it because it serves as a timeless piece of inspiration. Now, consider the human being. If we might be willing to treat a painting with such care and love—a painting worth a mere $269 million—how much more so should we treat ourself and other human beings, who have infinite value! As it is said at the end of every AA meeting: "Keep coming back. It works if you work it, *and work it 'cause you're worth it."*

The Dignity of Equality

The Torah spends a lot of time, with many verses, even chapters, dedicated to detailing ancestry lineages. Each of those lines of ancestry trace back to the same origin—Adam, the first human being. In this subtle way, the Torah is continually reminding us that we are all related. All of us are literally cousins, no matter what we look like. We are all *b'nai Adam*, literally the "children of Adam" (*adam* is also the word for "human being" in Hebrew). It is worth noting that modern science corroborates this religious concept. With genetic research, scientists have been able to identify a common ancestor and a male chromosome that all men on earth share. They call it the "Adam gene." They are also able to identify a common female ancestor and a female chromosome that all women on earth share. They call it the "Eve gene."

According to our Mishnah, the second reason God began all of humanity with only one person is "for the sake of peace among people, that one should not say to his or her fellow, 'My father is greater than your father'; and that heretics should not say, 'There are many powers in Heaven.'" That is, none of us can say that our father or ancestor is greater than another because we all ultimately share the same ancestor. We all share the same basic chromosome and genetic material. It is certainly true that different races evolved over time. Asians have thicker eyelids and slanted eyes because they evolved to contend with the terrible storms and cold climate on that part of the earth. People range in skin colors, including black, brown, red, yellow, and white, due to varying human migration patterns. Those who evolved in areas with more ultraviolet radiation produced more melanin and their skin darkened. But there is no inherent hierarchy of races, since we all are literally brothers and sisters. One simply cannot be a racist and take Judaism seriously. We all are equal and, therefore, we should refrain from fighting and power struggles.

The second part of the quotation—"and that heretics should not say, 'There are many powers in Heaven'"—could be interpreted to refer to religious equality. The quotation, referring to the creation of Adam by a single Source, demonstrates that different gods did not create different peoples with some gods being superior to other gods. Many of us may worship differently and understand the Divine in multiple ways, but none of us—non-Jew, nonbeliever, and Jews themselves—should make a claim of superiority based on religion because, ultimately, we are all derived from the same single Force of Life.

We must acknowledge, however, that Judaism, as a religion, is particularistic. That is, we have a distinct preference as to how we express our beliefs and values. The Jewish Sabbath is on Saturday, a particular day, and Jews observe it in a particular way. Jews pray using particular prayers. Jews are attached to the Land of Israel for particular reasons. Jews have particular holidays and life cycles. And these particularities are not arbitrary, but are integrated into a larger system of wise living. That being said, there is room for pluralism within Judaism as to how exactly we do these particular things, which is why there are different denominations. Moreover, because there is total intellectual freedom in Judaism, how we think about other people is for us to choose.

Judaism itself contends that there are seventy "faces" of Torah and each one is legitimate and equal.[4] There are many ways to live a holy life, many paths that can be simultaneously true, even if how they are expressed is different and seemingly contradictory. A genuinely religious person, who takes her spirituality seriously, will make no inherent judgment about others who are either Jewish or not Jewish. Of course, Jews are human beings and human beings are inherently flawed, so there are racist, sexist, ethnocentric, and bad people who happen to be Jews. And we must admit that Jewish religiosity does not necessarily correlate with moral fiber; Nachmanides, the great medieval commentator, points out that someone may be a "scoundrel with the permission of the Torah" (*naval bir'shut ha-Torah*) by observing the letter of the law without behaving in accordance with the spirit of its intent.[5] It is worth noting, however, that Jews do not outright proselytize; like the eleventh tradition of AA, Judaism's "public relations policy is based on attraction rather than promotion."[6] This principle denotes an inherent respect toward other religious paths and other ways of living, which Judaism—when at its best—also encourages.

Finally, one of the beautiful aspects of recovery in rehab centers and AA meetings is that there is very little judgment about each other's mistakes and past. Every person in recovery has done things of which they are not proud. However, everyone is there for a common purpose—sobriety and living a healthy and happy life. Alcoholism, as with any addiction, is an equal opportunity disease. It does not distinguish between race, religion, gender, sexual orientation, or socioeconomic status. Alcoholism and addiction hit every group equally. In chapter 2, the *Big Book* observes this very fact and expresses the inherent dignity of equality among the individuals in the group. And when there is an understanding of the dignity of equality, true community and fellowship can emerge:

> We are average Americans. All sections of this country and many of its occupations are represented, as well as many political, economic, social, and religious backgrounds. We are people who normally would not mix. But there exists among us a fellowship of friendliness, and an understanding which is indescribably wonderful.[7]

The Dignity of Uniqueness

Rabbi Sharon Brous, the spiritual leader of IKAR in Los Angeles, once asked a group to look around the room at the faces of others.[8]

She asked them to notice the differences among the faces, the color of the hair and the eyes, the curve of the eyebrows and the shape of the mouth, the nose, the cheekbones, the chin, the skin. Her point was for them to become aware of the incredible diversity that characterized each face. Even though the room was filled with people who seemed to be similar in race and ethnicity, there was still remarkable variety. We just have to look, really look. And that is just our faces; that is just what is on the outside. We can only imagine the exponentially greater internal—mental, emotional, and spiritual—variety and distinctiveness that each of us holds inside.

The point is that we are each unique. There was never another you or me, or any of us, and there never will be. There are certainly people who look alike and there are even identical twins. However, despite similarities in appearances, we know that no one is the same, nor will they ever be. Our Mishnah (Sanhedrin 4:5) teaches this point when offering its third answer as to why God started humanity with one person:

> Again to declare the greatness of the Holy One, blessed be God, for a person stamps out many coins with one seal, and they are all alike, but the King, the King of kings, the Holy One, blessed be God, stamps each person with the seal of Adam, and not one of them is like his or her fellow. Therefore each and every one is obligated to say, "For my sake the world was created."

When Adam was created, he was the only person in the world. He was totally unique and his experience in the world was inimitable. In a sense, the whole world was his. When we realize that each of us is unique, that there is no one else like us, we can begin to see that, even though we are not alone, we are as unique as Adam. Our experience in the world is also totally inimitable; no one else will experience the world as we do in our time and place, with the people around us, and with our biology and intellect. In other words, no one else has had nor will anyone else ever have our experience, simply because no one is created the same as anyone else. The dignity of our uniqueness rests on this truth, for only by recognizing our uniqueness do we gain the dignity of self-appreciation for who we are and what we contribute to the world. Each of us has our own place and our own purpose in this sea of life.

Moreover, once we gain our own dignity of uniqueness we begin to appreciate the uniqueness of others. Just as we have our own place and role in the world, so do others. The beauty of our world and our society is that we have the opportunity to shine our unique gift on others, as well as receive the gifts they offer. This process of teaching and learning is one that sharpens and refines the qualities that each of us already has. It is mutually beneficial.

The rabbis of the Midrash expound on this idea when they ask a question about revelation, the giving of the Torah at Mt. Sinai in the book of Exodus (chap. 20).[9] They wonder how it was that each person experienced and understood the exact same thing at the point of revelation. Did children experience revelation the same way as the elderly? Did the deaf and disabled experience revelation the same as the hearing and able? The Midrash claims that each person experienced revelation differently. Each of them understood it according to his or her own capacity. In other words, each of us holds our own unique piece of Torah and divine revelation that no other person has.

The beauty and purpose of life, as a unique individual, becomes much more apparent in light of this teaching. That is, if each of us is totally unique and exclusively holds a component of divine revelation in our soul—a piece of the truth—that helps to comprise the totality of revelation, then we should be talking to one another about it. We should be talking to each other about our truth, listening to each other's stories, and learning with each other so that we can assemble each of our distinct pieces of truth together and become complete together. We are given our uniqueness so that it will be shared with others—we are supposed to give it away in order for all of us to become whole.

Embracing Dignity

Rabbinic tradition, especially as explicated in Hasidism, holds that there are different levels of consciousness that the human being experiences. These include:

1. *nefesh*, unconscious bodily knowledge that regulates automatic functions, such as breathing

2. *ruach*, subconscious emotional knowledge, which is associated with our fears and instinctive responses

3. *neshamah*, self-awareness, wherein we are able to conduct introspection and distinguish between ourself and everything else

4. *chayah*, social awareness, which is characterized by comprehending the unified, interconnectedness of the whole universe

5. *yechidah*, spiritual immersion, which is an experience of the dissolution of the sense of self as a separate entity and a recognition that we are each suffused with the superconsciousness of the universe

These varying levels of consciousness reflect that, as human beings, we are both bound to the world and our physical experience and, at the same time, we are outside of our own being and the flow of life. In other words, unlike animals that are totally present in their physical experience, we do not constantly live in the moment-to-moment flow of life. Unlike animals, we have the ability to project an image of ourself outside of ourself and outside of the present moment. We are able to see ourself as a child, and we are able to see ourself growing old and dying. Animals do not do that. We are homo sapiens, the "species that knows," and we know that we know. We are conscious beings, both living in the present moment and watching ourself live it—both within the narrative of our lives and simultaneously writing it. We watch ourself move from the past toward the future, which, according to Søren Kierkegaard, the great existentialist philosopher, constitutes humankind's both terrifying and ennobling struggle.[10]

To illustrate this point, imagine a young teenage boy in an awkward stage, sitting in front of his phone debating with himself about calling a particularly attractive young lady. He finally musters the courage to pick up the phone, dial, and have a brief conversation. When he hangs up the phone, he reflects on his conversation and what he said. He then says to himself, "Oh my gosh, you are such an idiot! I can't believe I said that. How could she ever like a guy like me?" Notice what is happening here: He is giving himself a sort of internal spanking. He is both giving and receiving a punishment. That is, he watched himself call her, heard himself say what he said, and then, looking back at the interaction, he projects an image of which he does not approve. On the one hand, he is the strong, objective enforcer of punishment, while simultaneously being the weak, humiliated martyr.

From the Jewish perspective, this scenario falls within the central point of consciousness, which is called *neshamah*, marking our self-awareness. This is the level where we are able to step out of ourself and think about ourself as a separate, unique being. It is where the ego and self-esteem develop and express themselves. This level is indeed the pivot on which our overall consciousness determines our emotional and intellectual health and balance. If this *neshamah* level becomes overly attentive to our separateness from others, we become isolated, selfish, lonely, depressed, and angry. If, however, the *neshamah* level is able to open up to the realization that our own welfare is beneficial to others as well as to ourself, then there will be balance.

Let's return to our example of the teenage boy. If he could realize that alienating that part of himself and beating himself up does no good for his whole self, and that it only drags the rest of his character further down into depression, anger, and isolation, he would be able to grow from the experience and be of greater service to himself and, as a result, others. This level of self-awareness and consciousness is critical for developing and establishing healthy self-esteem. If we are unable to go beyond untamed, self-absorbed alienation, where we understand that there is a bigger image of the self to care for, we develop a very unhealthy ego, blind to the possibility of connection and immersed in broken seclusion. When we become self-absorbed and inflate a certain aspect of our self, the ego alone becomes the only concern, obsessing about how we are separate, rather than how we are connected. We tend to focus only on deficiencies rather than abundance, on chaos rather than peace, and on alienation rather than union. Of course, this concern is totally in our mind and, even though it is experienced as absolutely real, it is, in fact, an illusion—a story we tell ourself. This unhealthy wall of negativity—this denial of abundance, peace, and union—that we put up at this level of consciousness is the place from which the evil inclination or the *yetzer ha-ra* emerges (the following chapter discusses the evil inclination).

Accepting Our Dignities

As alcoholics and addicts, we often become numb to the emotional experience. We skillfully avoid it by isolating ourselves through the time and ritual of acquiring and using drugs and alcohol. We focus on our own small internal world, overlooking the impact our behavior has on others, as well as ourselves. We may be absolutely aware of how other people have hurt and wronged us, giving us even more reason to get loaded, yet oblivious to the weight of own actions or inaction. Along the way, we lose the connection to our own dignity, our own self-worth. We enjoy many "pity parties" about ourselves, wallowing in shame and worthlessness. Or we may blame others—parents, ex-lovers, employers, society at large—and delude ourselves into finding grandeur in our suffering. In either case, we deny our dignities. We are stuck behind the walls of our own self-imposed prison, denying our potential value and uniqueness. And in our inability to see our own worth, we deny the worth of others, the equality of all humanity.

Denying our dignities is the first step toward the last moments before the first drink, the first pill, or the first hit. It is when we say to ourself: "To hell with it all. Nothing really matters." Part of recovery and spiritual healing is coming back to terms with these dignities. And healthy and long-lasting recovery rests on our ability to accept our imperfections as part of our uniqueness so that we can let them go and allow ourself to rise to our higher consciousness—the part of ourself that recognizes our eternal, infinite worth.

Personal Reflections

Becoming a parent has had a profound effect on my view of life and myself. As a parent, I have had the amazing privilege of being able to see the world anew through my children's eyes. I've watched them squeal with joy and awe at their first encounter with the ocean. I've watched them learn new songs, and then sing them over and over. I've watched them go to their first baseball game and look in wonder as everyone stands to sing "Take Me Out to the Ballgame" during the seventh-inning stretch. I've watched them make mistakes and then experience the relief and power of being able to make amends. For them, the world is an adventure, a playground on which they are free to explore with their gifts of body and mind.

I have asked myself many times what I hope and pray for them in life. Do I want them to be successful, educated adults? Of course. Do I want them to be healthy and safe? Of course. I want them to have all that and more. But more than anything else, I want each of them to be grateful for their own self and their own life. That's because if they are not grateful for their own self and their own life, they will not be able to genuinely appreciate and enjoy any of those other things.

At some point in my life, I made a decision that I should be ashamed of myself. I began to believe that I wasn't good enough or smart enough and that no one really gave a damn about me. I believed that I couldn't rely on others because they would just disappoint me—because they really didn't care about me. I would have to take care of myself and nothing would come easily.

In my world, I wasn't grateful for anything because I was too absorbed in what separated me from others, worrying about the next problem I had to tackle. I was too mistrustful to believe that any gift I was given was sincere; it must end in disappointment somehow. I couldn't believe that I was genuinely worthy of anything or any love. So I stayed in my emotional shell. I couldn't experience gratitude because I had no gratitude for being me and being given the life and gifts I was given. I was a martyr and gave to others out of martyrdom.

Only in gratitude for myself could I truly have gratitude for anything else; otherwise, I was too self-absorbed. Once I found gratitude for myself—that I could digest food into energy, that I can think, learn, teach, love, and give and take pleasure—could I let go of my own self-absorption and focus my attention and appreciation on the world. Gratitude for myself isn't an ego boost, but rather a form of self-respect and dignity—the dignity and respect we all deserve. Once I own my own dignity, I can then respect the dignity of others.

Therefore, I pray for my girls to be grateful. If they can be grateful, I know that they will live a life of dignity and happiness no matter what their circumstances.

Chapter 4

The Evil Inclination

Now the serpent was the shrewdest of all the wild beasts that the Lord God had made. He said to the woman, "Did God really say: You shall not eat of any tree of the garden?" The woman replied to the serpent, "We may eat of the fruit of the other trees of the garden. It is only about fruit of the tree of the middle of the garden that God said: 'You shall not eat of it or touch it, lest you die.'" And the serpent said to the woman, "You are not going to die, but God knows that as soon as you eat of it your eyes will be opened and you will be like divine beings knowing good and bad." When the woman saw that the tree was good for eating and a delight to the eyes, and that the tree was a desirable source of wisdom, she took of its fruit and ate. (Genesis 3:1–6)

The Origin of "Evil"

The first thing to understand about the "sin" in the Garden of Eden is that it was not a sin. According to the story, the tree from which Adam and Eve ate was the Tree of Knowledge of Good and Bad, which grants moral conscience. Therefore, before they actually ate the fruit from the tree, they could not have known the difference between good and bad. They would not have known that listening to the serpent, eating from the tree, and disobeying God were actually bad things to do. What they did was not a sin because they simply did not know what they were doing. They merely exercised their free will.

Furthermore, the consequence for eating the fruit was not a punishment. God said, "[as for the Tree of Knowledge of Good and Bad], you must not eat of it; for as soon as you eat of it, you shall die." But they did eat the fruit of that tree. And they did not die—certainly not "as soon as" they ate of it, as God had said. Consequently, as a result of eating the fruit, rather than receiving a punishment, they had an awakening. Adam and Eve awakened to the fact that they would die and that they would suffer their curses of childbearing and hard work. They awakened to the fact that they could not live in the warm and sunny confines of the Garden, with the presence of God nearby, their protective parent. We might say that they died a figurative death, but only to be born again into another consciousness.

Outside the Garden

The story of the Garden of Eden is not a story of sin and punishment, but of coming of age. And coming of age, into adolescence and adulthood, is something with which we all contend. We come to the realization that we must go out on our own and leave the "garden." For many of us, because of the way in which we were raised, going out on our own is painful and difficult, and we feel naked, ashamed, and vulnerable. Ideally, when we are young and developing, our parents and caregivers will nurture us and support us through tough times. Eventually, through the modeling of the adults closest to us, we learn to self-nurture and self-support, and, when it comes time to go out on our own, presumably we have learned the skills and coping mechanisms to balance our lives. Many of us, however, do not achieve this ideal prior to adolescence and adulthood. Our parents and caregivers may have done the best they could with what they had, but it may not have been what we needed to leave the "garden" fully ready. Yet we have to leave anyway because of age, culture, and circumstance, and, sometimes, because we demand it.

When we depart into adolescence and adulthood, we discover a challenging world with many people trying to find their own happiness. We find ourself amid an array of delights and horrors, truths and lies, and pleasures and pains, and we are pulled in many different directions. Primarily, we are pulled in two directions: toward what is good and toward what is bad. These poles become complicated, however, because it is often hard to distinguish what is good from what is bad. What looks good or feels good may not actually be good, and what looks bad may not actually be bad. Furthermore, sometimes what we want for ourself is bad for us. We want to relax, but we need to work. We want pleasure, but the pleasure we seek may be unhealthy or dangerous. We want total freedom, but there are rules to follow. We want to feel strong and good, but we get sick and feel weak. We want to feel confident and fearless, but we get scared. We want fairness and justice, but life is often unfair and unjust. Life as an adolescent and adult is not like life in the "garden" at all.

Thus, we are caught on a narrow bridge between two opposing poles. Judaism teaches that each of us is imbued with these two poles in our psyches, referred to as impulses, urges, or inclinations. We have the inclination and capacity for both good and bad. We refer to the inclination toward bad or evil as the *yetzer ha-ra*. We refer to the part of ourself that is drawn toward the good as the *yetzer ha-tov*, the good inclination. It may be easier to define the *yetzer ha-tov* and the *yetzer ha-ra* by utilizing contemporary social psychologist Erich Fromm's definitions of good and evil. He says:

Good is the affirmation of life, the unfolding of man's powers. Virtue is responsibility toward his own existence. Evil constitutes the crippling of man's powers; vice is irresponsibility toward himself.[1]

That is to say, the *yetzer ha-tov* inclines us toward affirming our own existence in the place, time, and body through living to our greatest potential. Acting in life-affirming ways or performing "esteemable acts" is an expression of our virtue. On the other hand, the *yetzer ha-ra* inclines us toward denying our existence in this place, time, and body through living to our lowest potential. Life-denying acts and behaving self-destructively are our vices.

Living with both of these inclinations and knowing that we have them within us is a cause for great angst. In fact, we might say that the shame and vulnerability that Adam and Eve experienced once they ate from the Tree of Knowledge of Good and Bad is not only that they awoke to the fact that they must go out on their own, but also that they realized they are capable of doing bad, as well as good. We have that same experience; we know that we are capable of both good and bad. And there is an inherent potential shame to knowing the bad toward which we are inclined.

Suppressing versus Repressing the *Yetzer Ha-Ra*

To complicate matters more, however, our inclination toward bad is not actually all that bad. Judaism proclaims that everything that God creates is good, even the evil inclination, the *yetzer ha-ra*.[2] The truth is that it is difficult to define or name what is "evil" within us, when it is not really all that evil. Essentially, what draws us toward the bad, our evil inclination, is our impulse to self-alienate. When we separate ourself from others, the world, and even ourself—when all that matters to us is our own self and what we want in that moment—we are more likely to be drawn to do bad things. Take the following rabbinic parable as an example:

> Once, two men were traveling together on a boat ... One man casually takes out a hand drill and begins to drill a hole under his seat. The other man is startled and asks of him, "What are you doing? Don't you know that you're going to sink the

boat?" The first man says simply, "What, I'm not drilling on your side. What's the big deal? It's not my problem."[3]

In this scenario, the one who is drilling in the boat is so ignorant, so self-absorbed, that he is incapable of seeing how his actions are affecting someone else—someone sitting right beside him. That ignorance functions like a veil, concealing not only how what he is doing will harm another, but also ultimately how what he is doing will harm himself (he's in the boat, too, and will sink along with his companion). This blindness that we can experience to the interests of anyone or anything else around ourself, and even to our own greater self-interests beyond the moment, is the *yetzer ha-ra*, the evil inclination, because it usually results in negative outcomes. The power of the *yetzer ha-ra* is continuously raised in Judaism and it should not be underestimated, because we all have it.

How, then, is the *yetzer ha-ra* not all that bad? Sometimes, in order to survive or achieve something, we have to be a bit focused on ourself and driven by our own needs. The rabbis explicitly point this out, saying: "If not for the *yetzer ha-ra* [the evil inclination], no one would build a house, marry, have children, or engage in a trade."[4] The point here is that there is a time to work toward our self-interests for the sake of satisfying the needs of survival and safety, love and procreation, and prosperity. From time to time we need to take care of ourself and accomplish certain things in life. This drive stems from the same alienating, self-absorbed *yetzer ha-ra* that causes us to do harm.

Therefore, the task is not to completely repress the *yetzer ha-ra* and destroy it (which is impossible anyway), but to suppress it. As the rabbis teach:

Let not a Jew proclaim: "It is against my nature to eat pork; it is against my nature to desire an illicit sexual union." What, then, shall he proclaim? He should say: "It is surely possible for me to desire pork; it is possible for me to desire illicit sex.

But, alas, what can I do when God in heaven has set His decree upon me to refrain."[5]

Thus, instead of repressing our urges, the task is to be aware of those thoughts and feelings, and then to control them so that they do not run amok and become part of our character, resulting in perpetual self-centered callousness. If those thoughts mount up unacknowledged, we are more likely to express them in action, causing harm. Judaism teaches that either we become our mind's master and the master of our evil inclination, or it masters us. As the sage Ben Zoma rhetorically asked: "Who is strong? One who controls [i.e., not eliminates] his *yetzer ha-ra*, evil inclination."[6]

Identifying the *Yetzer Ha-Ra*

The self-alienating *yetzer ha-ra* is easy to identify once we have done something wrong. The harmful actions speak for themselves. But we must be aware of the fact that the actual behavior is the result of the toll that the *yetzer ha-ra* has taken on our psyche over time. In other words, the *yetzer ha-ra* begins as an impulse, which then leads to a way of thinking and feeling. Then, when the opportunity arises for expression of those thoughts and feelings in action, we witness the evidence of the *yetzer ha-ra*.

The ego is the place from which the *yetzer ha-ra* emerges and it has essentially two sides, both of which make up the same "coin." The ego is concerned with the self, and a healthy ego results in healthy self-esteem, balancing humility and pride. Notice that humility and pride are both self-focused. Pride prompts us to compare ourself with others and point out when we do something well or how we are superior to others. Humility prompts us to compare ourself with others and point out how others do something well or how we are inferior to others. A healthy ego balances these claims and enables both pride and humility to motivate us, while being realistic and cooperative. When the ego is not properly balanced, humility morphs into humiliation and pride transforms into arrogance. In either case, the ego will become self-absorbed and block out the needs of others, and, because it is so self-absorbed, it will do so even to its own detriment. This is how the *yetzer ha-ra* becomes manifest.

The Depressive Ego

The *12 and 12* of Alcoholics Anonymous, in its own way, also identifies the experience of the unhealthy ego and emergence of the two primary dispositions of the *yetzer ha-ra*. It speaks of the depressive disposition and the grandiose disposition. Regarding the former, it says:

> If temperamentally we are on the depressive side, we are apt to be swamped with guilt and self-loathing. We wallow in this messy bog, often getting misshapen and painful pleasure out it. As we morbidly pursue this melancholy activity, we may sink to such a point of despair that nothing but oblivion looks possible as a solution. Here, of course, we have lost perspective, and therefore all genuine humility. For this is pride in reverse. This is not a moral inventory at all; it is the very process by which the depressive has so often been led to the bottle and extinction.[7]

We see here clearly that the depressive side is actually not a form of humility at all, but a distortion of it. In this case, we take a selfish, morbid pleasure in self-flagellation and self-deprecation. We are not really thinking about others at all, but enjoying our "pity party." Interestingly, Judaism warns of the self-flagellating persona and how it can manifest in a false sense of religious self-righteousness—when people incline toward a false sense of piety.

> The Maggid of Koznitz said to a man who wore nothing but a sack and fasted from one Sabbath to the next, "The Evil Inclination is tricking you into that sack. He who pretends to fast

... but secretly eats a little something every day, is spiritually better off than you, for he is only deceiving others, while you are deceiving yourself.[8]

In the case of alcoholics and addicts, self-imposed humiliation becomes an excuse to drink or use. We impose on ourselves a sense of shame that no one can endure without release. Natural joy vanishes; there is only isolation. Under the delusion of depression, we swear that no one can save us and, even if they could, they would choose not to. There is no one to trust, no one to talk to, and there is no point in coming clean and making amends, but there is the comforting lie (and we know it is a lie, which compounds our shame) that the drink or drug will make it okay for today. Depressives are able to rationalize all sorts of destructive behaviors based on morbid self-deprecation.

The Grandiose Ego

And then there is the grandiose disposition of the *yetzer ha-ra*, of which the *12 and 12* notes:

> If, however, our natural disposition is inclined to self-righteousness or grandiosity, our reaction will be just the opposite.... We also clutch at another wonderful excuse for avoiding an inventory [i.e., a moral inventory of our resentments and personal accountability]. Our present anxieties and troubles, we cry, are caused by the behavior of other people—people who *really* need a moral inventory. We firmly believe that if only they'd treat us better, we'd be all right. Therefore we think our indignation is justified and reasonable—that our resentments are the "right kind." We aren't the guilty ones. *They* are![9]

In this case, we see pride morph into arrogance. We become so self-absorbed that we are unable to see our own responsibility or accountability in these relationships. The self-absorption has hardened the ego to a point of impenetrability. It is the hardheartedness of the Pharaoh that would not let the slaves go free. There is no willingness to cooperate, comply, or change. There is no open-mindedness to learn more. There are no feelings that matter other than our feelings. It is a superiority complex whereby we feel entitled to break the rules, to gossip about others, to give ourself an unwarranted raise or permission to have an affair. And once alcohol and drugs enter the system of those of us with a grandiose disposition, explosive anger is often near at hand.

Keep in mind that everyone has a *yetzer ha-ra*, not just alcoholics and addicts. Everyone is capable of carrying either the depressive or the grandiose temperament. Indeed, we may recognize such types all around us—in our workplace or in our families—and they may never have even had a drink or taken a drug in their life. Also, we need to recognize that, sometimes, we may switch from one disposition to the other, depending on the circumstances. Yet, in the end, the *yetzer ha-ra* is simply part of our mental, emotional, and spiritual composition. It is part of being human and it is an indiscriminate, equal-opportunity force, no matter what our gender, race, culture, sexual orientation, religion, or socioeconomic status, or whether or not we are addicted.

And, just as much as anyone else, it affects the intelligent and well educated, too—no one can outthink the *yetzer ha-ra* and no one is ever entirely free of its influence. As the Talmud declares: "The greater the person, the greater the *yetzer ha-ra*."[10] Regarding the intelligent alcoholic, a humorous anecdote is told by a graduate student speaking to Dr. Dan Anderson, the then-president of the Hazelden Foundation, a renowned addiction treatment center, and a leading expert on addiction. It illustrates the tendency of intelligent addicts to be just as susceptible to the *yetzer ha-ra* as those with the two aforementioned dispositions:

> "Why is it," I asked, "that even intelligent alcoholics can get trapped in denial of their alcoholism? Is it because of grandiosity—they think that they can do anything to their bodies and survive, they think they are 'too smart' to be 'alcoholic'? Or is

it because of self-loathing—they despise themselves and feel they deserve to die, if they are alcoholics?"

"Ernie, Ernie, Ernie," Dan groaned with a patient smile. "The alcoholic's problem is not that he thinks, 'I am very special.' Nor is the alcoholic's problem that he thinks, 'I am a worm.' The alcoholic's problem is that he is *convinced*: 'I am a very special worm.'"[11]

Elevating Evil

Although the *yetzer ha-ra* manifests itself in general ways, it expresses itself in distinct ways within each of us. As Rabbi Israel Salanter, the founder of the *Mussar* movement in Orthodox Judaism, remarked, "No person is like another when it comes to transgression."[12] However, rather than seeing these transgressions, these expressions of the *yetzer ha-ra*, as pitiful spiritual deficits, Judaism teaches that they may be opportunities to grow. The founder of Hasidism, the Baal Shem Tov, taught that we should elevate our alien and foreign thoughts, rather than rejecting them. In other words, instead of rejecting them as "bad," we should pay attention to them because they can teach us something about ourself.

In fact, our specific spiritual defects that are unique to us teach us about our purpose here. Each of us has our own distinct spiritual mission here on earth, or our *tikkun* (spiritual corrective). A part of our soul needs growth. Imagine the soul as a multifaceted diamond with each facet representing a different spiritual attribute. Our spiritual goal is to polish each of the facets. Many of them are already polished early in life, while others are only partially polished. Those that are not yet polished project outward as our *yetzer ha-ra*, expressing itself in our behavior. If we pay attention to the "dirty" behavior, we are better able to identify the underlying grime that produced it. And once we identify the underlying cause of our *yetzer ha-ra*, elevating it to our consciousness, we are then equipped to consciously make better decisions, thereby polishing that facet. Rabbi Moses Chaim Luzzatto, the great eighteenth-century ethicist, explicitly states:

[Humankind is] placed between wholeness and deficiency, with the power to earn his wholeness. Man must earn this wholeness, however, through his own free will.... Man's inclinations are therefore balanced between good and evil, and he is not compelled toward either of them. He has the power of choice and is able to choose either side knowingly and willingly.[13]

We can choose good over bad. We can control our *yetzer ha-ra*, but first we must be willing to honestly study ourself and come to know those deviant urges, thoughts, and feelings. If we do not accept these imperfect sides of ourself, we are resisting learning about what may be our spiritual purpose in the world. If we deny this side of ourself, which is just as real and just as much a part of our humanity as the good, we are limiting the authentic, intended choices that we make in life. Like children, we are expected to make mistakes. However, we are supposed to learn from them so that we do not repeat them. If we do not take an honest internal moral inventory that elevates our *yetzer ha-ra* to our consciousness, we are simply going to go in circles, chasing our own tail. A Hasidic story helps make this point:

Once some disciples of Rabbi Pinchas ceased talking in embarrassment when he entered the house of study. When he asked them what they were talking about, they said: "Rabbi, we were saying how afraid we are that the *yetzer ha-ra* will pursue us."

"Don't worry," he replied. "You have not gotten high enough for it to pursue you. For the time being, you are still pursuing it."[14]

Being honest with ourself and accepting our imperfections are the first spiritual steps in recovering our unique sense of self and discovering our spiritual purpose in the world.

Personal Reflections

When I was growing up, I wanted to be loved. I wanted to feel connected to my family, friends, and the world. I wanted to be a good boy and do the right thing. I experienced chaos in my family through the upheaval of moving to different cities and schools, as well as rampant addiction and divorce among my siblings. Through it all, my impulse was always to try to bring peace. I certainly never wanted to hurt the people I loved.

So how did I find myself absorbed in addiction and doing destructive things that affected both those I care about and myself? It seems surreal that I did what I did, even to me. I compare the experience to one of those werewolf movies where people wake up in the morning to find the city ravaged. Someone then says, "The werewolf was here last night." I reply, "Oh my! Somebody needs to stop that werewolf. He's terrible!" Then one morning I wake up to find everything trashed again, but this time I see the blood on my own hands. I realize that I am the werewolf! I'm overcome with fear and shame. I fear that I can't control myself, that I am powerless to rein in my own destructive nature.

One of the hardest things that I have had to accept is that I have a bad side to myself. I think bad thoughts and feel hurtful feelings. Along with my goodness and love for life and people, I have urges toward anger, hate, and fear. I continue to work on accepting this part of myself. I don't see myself as tainted with sin. Rather, I see that I struggle with the challenges of life: with injustice and unfairness, with insecurity (financial and otherwise), and with loneliness. I work to accept these feelings as part of life, as opposed to what I used to do, which was to deny them through drinking.

I have learned that I can live with hurtful feelings and not only cope with them but also learn and grow from them. If I don't accept and learn from bad thoughts and feelings, if I just repress them because they are too uncomfortable, then they will eventually blossom and explode into my beast—my werewolf. For me, the only way to happiness is to be honest with myself about my own thoughts and feelings, knowing that they may be odd or depraved. I try to identify where they originated and confront them from there. I know that I can hold those thoughts and feelings without acting on them. Those thoughts and feelings are not worth violating my integrity or disconnecting from others, because deep down—in the deepest part of my core—all I really yearn for is connection to myself and others grounded in honest authenticity. All I really want is intimacy without losing a sense of my own individual uniqueness.

Chapter 5

Judaism and Alcohol

A Complicated Relationship

> Do not gaze at wine when it is red, when it sparkles in the cup and goes down smoothly. For in the end it bites like a poisonous snake and stings like a viper. (Proverbs 23:31–32)

O ne of the most poignant sections of the AA *Big Book* is at the start of chapter 3 when it characterizes the alcoholic:

No person likes to think he is bodily and mentally different from his fellows. Therefore, it is not surprising that our drinking careers have been characterized by countless vain attempts to prove we could drink like other people. The idea that somehow, someday he will control and enjoy his drinking is the great obsession of every abnormal drinker. The persistence of this illusion is astonishing. Many pursue it into the gates of insanity or death.

... All of us felt at times that we were regaining control, but such intervals—usually brief—were inevitably followed by still less control, which led to pitiful and incomprehensible demoralization. We are convinced to a man that alcoholics of our type are in the grip of a progressive illness....

We are men who have lost their legs; they never grow new ones....

Here are some of the methods we have tried. Drinking beer only, limiting the number of drinks, never drinking in the morning, drinking only at home, never having it in the house, never drinking during business hours, drinking only at parties, switching from scotch to brandy, drinking only natural wines, agreeing to resign if ever drunk on the job, taking a trip, not taking a trip, swearing off forever (with and without a solemn oath), taking more physical exercise, reading inspirational books, going to health farms and sanitariums, accepting voluntary commitment to asylums—we could increase the list ad infinitum.[1]

For recovery to begin, alcoholics must understand that "no real alcoholic *ever* recovers control" of his drinking. The Narcotics Anonymous literature, referring to drinking and using, puts it succinctly: "If you are like us you know that one [drink or drug] is too much and a thousand never enough."[2] Yet, despite this knowledge, the fantasy persists in the mind of the alcoholic that he will be able to drink normally. He has tried controlling it, employing every method under the sun to "drink like a gentleman," but, as one AA member said when referring to the reading selection above as the "pickle page": "Once a pickle, always a pickle. There's no going back to being a cucumber."

In this light, Jewish alcoholics face a particular challenge. Jewish holidays, life-cycle events, and every Friday night as Shabbat (the Sabbath) is celebrated, these events are sanctified with a cup of wine.

Jewish children learn of the Friday night blessing over the wine in preschool, as well as the four mandatory cups of wine on Passover, and the frivolous custom of becoming intoxicated on Purim. Of course, there are also multiple occasions for a *l'chayim* (literally, "to life," referring to a toast over a shot of liquor). Some people like to joke that Judaism not only accepts drinking alcohol as a norm, but even encourages it. Furthermore, many synagogues leverage the appeal of alcohol by offering Torah study classes while drinking, marketing them with titles such as "Torah and Toasts" or "Learning with a *L'Chayim*." Unfortunately, there are also some despicable synagogue establishments that openly serve alcohol to teenagers and underage drinkers in hopes of building attendance among the youth.[3]

There is no doubt that drinking wine and liquor is a part of Judaism. The first prohibition against drinking wine and liquor in the Torah itself applies only to the priestly cult.[4] Since the priests were responsible for conducting sacred rites, they could not be impaired and unable to "distinguish between the holy and the profane." The second prohibition applies to a special sect called the Nazirites, who would take a voluntary vow of abstention, including abstaining from intoxicants, abstaining from eating or drinking anything made with grapes (including wine and vinegar), and cutting their hair.[5] But none of us is either a Temple priest or a Nazirite, so these laws exist only in the vaults of history. They now symbolize an almost impossible ideal of ascetic piety.

What most Jews seem to know about drinking in the Jewish tradition is that there is a lot of it. Jewish sources most often referenced about drinking justify it and even glorify it, such as the following one from the Hebrew Bible:

> He causes the grass to grow for the cattle, and vegetation for the labor of man, so that he may bring forth food from the earth, and *wine which makes man's heart glad* [emphasis mine], so that he may make his face glisten with oil, and food which sustains man's heart. (Psalms 104:14–15)

And from rabbinic literature:

> No rejoicing before God is possible except with wine. (B. Talmud, *Pesachim* 109a)

These Jewish sources are not wrong. There are certainly benefits to drinking alcohol. If there were not benefits, no alcoholic would have started drinking in the first place. Alcohol does "make man's heart glad." Alcohol loosens the mind and can help facilitate joy and camaraderie. It is accepted in Judaism that drinking alcohol together with friends and family is a way for Jews to bond (not to merely pass the time) and, as a twentieth-century rabbi, Kalman Shapira, put it: "[D]rinking also loosens and rouses the animal nature—which adds passion and vigor to our efforts."[6]

Given the positive Jewish accounting of drinking, what is a Jewish alcoholic to do? Again, as the texts cited above point out, drinking works to relieve anxiety and add passion and vigor. But we also know, as the *Big Book* explicitly and correctly states, that an alcoholic cannot control her drinking. She cannot have a glass of wine on Friday night because she will not stop at a glass. As soon as she has one drink and the initial relief and euphoria hit, she will be unable to stop obsessing until she has another drink and another, until she passes out. No drink is too strong for her. She cannot have the four cups on Passover. Drinking does work for the alcoholic at first, until it becomes an obsession of the mind. It works until it becomes the only way she knows how to experience relief. It works until it becomes the center of her life and everything else comes toppling down. It works until it starts to slowly destroy everything in her life.

A Source of Depravity

What is not often taught about alcohol in Jewish settings is that the rabbis of old were very well aware of the destructive power of alcohol. Referencing back to the Garden of Eden and the fruit of the Tree of

Knowledge of Good and Bad, one tradition claims that the tree was a vine and Eve and Adam ate grapes:

> We have been taught that Rabbi Meir said: The tree whose fruit Adam ate was a vine, for nothing brings as much distress to humans as wine. (B. Talmud, *Sanhedrin* 70a)

In Judaism, the most common fruit associated with the Tree of Knowledge of Good and Bad is the fig. This is based on a logical deduction because once Adam and Eve eat from that tree, they realize that they are naked and they cover themselves with fig leaves. Therefore, it must have been a fig tree. Other traditions claim it was a citron tree (*etrog*), which has great symbolism in Judaism, especially in terms of its association with the fall harvest festival Sukkot. Of course, the apple represents another tradition and is often the artist's choice in depicting the scene in Eden. Here, however, Rabbi Meir, a second-century sage, teaches that it was a vine. In this case, he relates the difficulties and curses that humankind experiences as a result of eating the fruit from the tree. Therefore, the fruit that brings humankind difficulty and curses is the vine, which leads us to drink wine.

And how does wine make life more difficult, according to the rabbis?

> As wine enters each and every part of a human's body it grows lax, and his mind is confused. Once wine enters, reason leaves. (Midrash, Numbers Rabbah 10:8)

Accordingly, even though wine has merits in Judaism and is used in sanctifying sacred days and occasions, we begin to see that Jewish leaders caution against drinking alcohol. As the alcoholic knows all too well, when we drink we lose our capacity to make sound decisions. Although our judgment may be poor when we're sober, the more and the longer we drink, the more irrational, selfish, and destructive choices we make. Undoubtedly, drunken thinking is not our best thinking.

Perhaps the most elaborate depiction of the rabbinic awareness that drinking can cause problems comes in a medieval legend portraying Noah and Satan (Satan in Judaism is the prosecuting angel against humanity in the celestial realm, not the devil). The text is a direct response to the quotation from the book of Psalms above, which says that "wine makes man's heart glad":

> When Noah began planting, Satan came by, stationed himself before him, and asked, "What are you planting?" Noah said, "It's fruit. Whether fresh or dried, it is sweet, and from it wine is made, which gladdens a person's heart." Satan replied, "Would you like the two of us, me and you, to plant it together?" "Very well," said Noah.
>
> What did Satan do? He brought a ewe lamb and slaughtered it over the vine; then he brought a lion, which he likewise slaughtered over the vine; then a monkey, which he also slaughtered over the vine; and finally a pig, which he again slaughtered over the vine. And with the blood dripping from them, he watered the vineyard.
>
> The charade was Satan's way of saying that when a person drinks one cup of wine, he acts like a ewe lamb, humble and meek. When he drinks two, he becomes as mighty as a lion and proceeds to brag extravagantly, saying, "Who is like me?" When he drinks three or four cups, he becomes like a monkey, hopping about, dancing, giggling, and uttering obscenities in public, without realizing what he is doing. Finally, when he becomes blind drunk, he is like a pig, wallowing in mud and coming to rest among refuse. (Midrash *Tanhuma*, Noah 13)

This is a powerful text because it tells us that wine, particularly its power to inebriate, is the design of Satan, the angel of the *yetzer ha-ra*, the evil inclination. It also employs creative metaphor to compare the experience of drinking to the slow spiral into depravity and oblivion.

Alcoholics can certainly relate to each stage that is described, none of which is flattering. What is most powerful about this text, however, is that it provides an outside perspective on the drunk. In other words, it depicts how others see the drunk as he progresses in his drinking.

Alcoholics have the uncanny ability to be totally unaware of the effect of their drinking, both emotionally and practically, on those around them. We suffer from a sort of selective amnesia, where we distort the memory of our drinking episodes, so that they do not appear as bad as they were. As one AA member put it, "I always remember the fun times drinking, not the last, miserable time drinking." Thus, we deceive ourselves and justify another run to the liquor store or bar. As the text points out, we may feel like a "lion," master of our domain, when, in fact, we are acting aggressively and stupid—and everybody but us knows and sees it. Again, the *Big Book* offers insight:

> We are unable to bring into our conscious with sufficient force of memory the suffering and humiliation of even a week or a month ago....
>
> The almost certain circumstances that follow taking even a glass of beer do not crowd into the mind to deter us. If these thoughts occur, they are hazy and readily supplanted with the old threadbare idea that this time we shall handle ourselves like other people. There is a complete failure of the kind of defense that keeps one from putting his hand on a hot stove.[7]

In sum, we see that Judaism has a complicated relationship with wine and drinking liquor. Clearly, wine and its accompanying blessing (*borei p'ri ha-gafen*) are critical for sacred occasions. That being said, the same blessing can be made over grape juice. The real challenge for the Jewish alcoholic is to bring to the fore an as-yet unrecognized problem in the Jewish community, which is alcoholism. Alcoholism is as much an issue among Jews as it is among any religious or ethnic group. Whether it is by alcoholics themselves, family and friends of alcoholics, therapists and counselors, or clergy, more education about the disease of alcoholism is necessary in Jewish communal institutions. The Jewish community should embrace alcoholics and addicts—we are your relatives, your friends, your colleagues, and even your leaders. Judaism is not only for the well; it is also for the sick. Judaism and the Jewish community can be a source of strength for those struggling with alcoholism and addiction, and those touched by it. First, we need to open our eyes to it and become sensitive to the suffering that this disease causes, so that no alcoholic or addict feels ashamed for choosing grape juice over wine.

Getting Loaded on Purim

A Hasidic teaching says that we can learn three things from small children: how to keep busy, how to cry for what we need, and how to laugh and be cheerful.[8] What do these three things have in common? They tell us that children are able to become completely absorbed in what they do. The mind of the child is free; it is not constrained by the responsibilities, expectations, or complexities of life. Engrossed in each moment, children busy themselves with anything of interest; they cry out with the wholeness of their hearts and laugh with every fiber of their being. This same freedom and exuberance inform the spirit of the Jewish holiday of Purim. It is the one day of the year that we are not just given permission, but mandated, to let go of restraint. We express this wild abandon by putting on masks to hide our true faces, but ironically- -and Purim is all about ironies—hiding behind masks enables us to exhibit normally concealed countenances.

At some point during Purim, as part of the feast or in a separate celebration, the holiday takes on the nature of a carnival.[9] Costumes, role-playing, and drunkenness are not merely permitted, but encouraged. During the Greco-Roman period (332 BC–395 CE), theater became very popular. Actors commonly wore masks portraying the gods, especially the Greek god Dionysus and the Roman god Bacchus, the respective gods of wine, who also presided over communication between the living and dead. Masks and costumes enabled actors to better portray comic roles, such as jesters or outrageous and ridiculous representations of the opposite sex. Also during this period, masquerading became a prominent part of carnivals and parades. Such processions had been conducted as far back as the times of ancient Egypt and originated as a way to mark the changing of seasons. They eventually were used to express the upending of earthly order, especially social order, becoming a setting in which people mocked society. The rich dressed as the poor, the poor as the rich, and the wise as fools. Although a sense of the supernatural remained, a comic atmosphere emerged and grew throughout the Middle Ages and the European Renaissance.

Drunkenness was a key element in this release of inhibitions. In Greek theater, for example, not only did the actors who portrayed Dionysus become intoxicated, but so did the audience. At medieval carnivals, raucousness was standard behavior, highlighted by blatant immodesty, sexual abandon, unbridled gluttony, and a general "howling at the wind." In later centuries, carnivals such as the New Orleans Mardi Gras and the Brazilian Carnival have served as more than a toppling of social order and release of inhibition. They express intense artistic creativity and, despite the varying social strata of the participants, a communal oneness.

On some level, Purim shares many of the attributes of theater and carnival. Embedded in the story of Esther and Mordecai are irony, comedy, and the overturning of social order. The story begins by masking the attributes of each character. As the scroll and the plot unfurl, the total accumulation of one ironic event after another results in an unexpected final outcome. The reversal of the fate of the characters is such that what could have been a tragedy becomes a comedy. The lowly Jews become powerful, the king and his senior minister are made out to be fools, and near annihilation of the Jewish community turns to triumph.

It's Not about Getting Loaded

Drunkenness has long been a condoned custom of Purim frivolity. The Talmud offers the authoritative opinion that we should become intoxicated on Purim until we are no longer able to distinguish (*ad delo yada*) between "cursed be Haman" and "blessed be Mordecai."[10] Yet, as Rabbi Alexander Ziskind of Grodnow wrote in the eighteenth century, the Talmud does not explicitly use the word *lehishtaker* (to become drunk), an observation that teaches us we should drink just enough to lighten the heart. Rabbi Ziskind says that because the Jewish people have so often been burdened with sadness, just a little bit of wine is appropriate to help achieve the spiritual mood of thanksgiving and joy required on Purim.[11]

The critical point here is that the purpose of the drinking on Purim is to be joyous. But what if drinking does not bring us joy? What if it destroys our life? The most significant authors of codes of Jewish law, including Maimonides, Joseph Karo (*Shulchan Arukh*), Moses Isserles (*Mapa*), and Israel Meir Kagan (aka the "Chofetz Chayim"; *Mishnah Berurah*), understand that drinking is not its own *mitzvah*, separate from general feasting. In other words, we should eat and be happy, and if drinking is suitable for that, then drink a little. If not, do not drink. In any case, they add that *no one should drink more than he or she is used to*. These are key points, because we can fulfill all our Purim observances without drinking at all, especially if we are in recovery, and therefore not used to drinking. One rabbinic commentator says explicitly:

> We are not obligated to become inebriated and degrade ourselves due to our joy [on Purim]. We are not obligated to engage in a *simchah* (joyous occasion) of frivolity and foolishness. Rather it should lead to a *simchah* of enjoyment, which should lead to love of God and thankfulness for the miracles He has performed for us.[12]

Judaism and its practices are essentially intended to remind us, to cue us and direct our energy toward the infinite potential and beauty of life. For some, having a bit to drink on the holiday of Purim, which commemorates the toppling of order, and allowing our inner feelings to emerge, can be joyful. For the alcoholic, however, a drink on Purim is a death sentence. The Jewish tradition has wisely evolved, making it unequivocally clear that there is no reason or obligation to drink or become intoxicated on any occasion. As the commentator above implies, there is a spirit to these customs and practices. In fact, sometimes we need to go beyond the letter of the law (*lifnim mishurat ha-din*) or the custom itself to ensure that we are tapping into the spirit of the law, to be thankful and connect with God. Drinking and using will not accomplish that for us, so we are exempt.

Personal Reflections

I believe it was the twentieth-century theologian Abraham Joshua Heschel who said: "Judaism is caught not taught." I interpret that to mean that what we learn about Judaism is not just what people say but what people do. For example, if parents and teachers say that Judaism teaches that we should judge others' character by what they do rather than by what they look like, but then they themselves are constantly judging people by appearances, we ultimately learn that Judaism says it's okay to judge people by appearances. The same concept might also apply to how we treat and talk about alcoholism and addiction.

Jews like to say that we are an accepting people. After all, we were slaves, alienated, and subjugated throughout history, so we are compassionate to others. In my experience, I have found a lot of ignorance and denial in the Jewish community about alcoholism and addiction. There are very few Jewish institutions that serve addicts. Rarely do rabbis speak from the pulpit about the disease of addiction, even though we know that there are a lot of families touched by and struggling with alcoholism and addiction.

In fact, there is a lot of drinking that goes on in the name of Judaism without context or comment. There's drinking on Shabbat and even wild drinking on Simchat Torah and Purim. There's a line in the Talmud that says we should get intoxicated on Purim. Many ignore the fact that, immediately following that one line, the Talmud tells a story of two rabbis—Rabbah and Zeira—having a Purim feast. They become intoxicated and Rabbah cuts Zeira's throat. The next day Rabbah prays and revives Zeira. The next Purim Rabbah invites Zeira back for another Purim feast, to which Zeira replies: "One cannot count on a miracle happening every time."[13] The story is a cautionary tale, tempering the idea that we should indiscriminately get intoxicated.

When I began to accept myself as an alcoholic, I felt terrified to tell anybody about it. I still worry about it (even as I put these thoughts in print). Granted, I am a rabbi and I know that my learning and title carry an additional burden of Jewish symbolism. But I am still a human being. I am reminded that there are plenty of things that rabbis have done that have been reprehensible. Rabbis have committed adultery; they have cheated and stolen money; they have slandered, lied, and gossiped; they have supported unethical political policies, such as slavery and segregation; they have denied women and the gay community their rights—certainly their equal status in the eyes of the Jewish tradition. Alcoholism and addiction, however, seem to hold their own unspoken taboo in the Jewish community.

What I know for myself now is that I will not contribute to Jewish ignorance about my disease. Neither will I commit my own pious hypocrisy, wielding my Judaism as a weapon against those who do wrong or suffer. Ultimately, alcoholism and addiction cause suffering, and the insane behavior of alcoholics and addicts is our way of crying out in pain, seeking to alleviate the suffering, even if only temporarily. When I reflect on my Judaism and my alcoholism, I become impassioned to do what I can to help those in my community who suffer as I have and do. My Judaism is not separate from my addiction and recovery, but integrated into it. My Judaism defers to compassion over castigation, mercy over spite, and love over punishment. We can only arrive at such compassion and love if we properly educate ourself and face our natural human imperfections.

Part II

The Covenant of Recovery— Spirituality in Action

Aligning Jewish Spirituality with AA

The world rests on three things—on Torah, on prayer, and on deeds of loving-kindness. (Mishnah, *Avot* 1:2)

Alcoholics Anonymous is a program of recovery based on spiritual action. Its declaration is: "The spiritual life is not a theory—*we have to live it*."[1] In addiction, action trumps thought because we learn that our thoughts and feelings are fleeting and untrustworthy counsel for what we want and need most in life. What we do and how we act are the best measures of our spirit. Therefore, a program of recovery consists of honestly participating in activities that embody a spiritual approach. As the book of *Narcotics Anonymous* clearly states: "There is one thing more than anything else that will defeat us in our recovery; this is an attitude of indifference or intolerance toward spiritual principles. Three of these that are indispensable are honesty, open-mindedness, and willingness. With these we are well on our way."[2]

Interestingly, the suggested "program" of both Alcoholics and Narcotics Anonymous is only delineated through the 12 Steps, which, at first glance, do not necessarily make for a clear program. A program is a specific set of behaviors designed to achieve a specific desired result. So, our question is this: What are the components of the steps that make up a program? When we look carefully at the 12 Steps of Alcoholics Anonymous, we can identify four primary actions and experiences that cultivate spirituality and foster recovery: study, prayer, repentance, and service. These four basic components of recovery are strongly aligned with principal Jewish spiritual values and practices. As we list these four actions and experiences in the following chapters, we will also look to align them with corresponding AA steps.

The 12 Steps are:

1. We admitted we were powerless over alcohol—that our lives had become unmanageable.

2. Came to believe that a Power greater than ourselves could restore us to sanity.

3. Made a decision to turn our will and our lives over to the care of God *as we understood Him*.

4. Made a searching and fearless moral inventory of ourselves.

5. Admitted to God, to ourselves, and to another human being the exact nature of our wrongs.

6. Were entirely ready to have God remove all these defects of character.

7. Humbly asked Him to remove our shortcomings.

8. Made a list of all persons we had harmed, and became willing to make amends to them all.

9. Made direct amends to such people wherever possible, except when to do so would injure them or others.

10. Continued to take personal inventory and when we were wrong promptly admitted it.

11. Sought through prayer and meditation to improve our conscious contact with God, *as we understood Him*, praying only for knowledge of His will for us and the power to carry that out.

12. Having had a spiritual awakening as the result of these Steps, we tried to carry this message to alcoholics, and to practice these principles in all our affairs.

Chapter 6

Study— *Talmud Torah*

When you are engaged in Torah, both in study and in
spiritual practice, you and God are one.

—Rabbi Schneur Zalman of Liadi

O f all of the Jewish practices, Torah study (or *Talmud Torah*)
stands above the rest as the most discussed and revered. As the
Talmud famously declares, "The study of Torah is greater than all
other *mitzvot* [Jewish values and practices] put together."[1] But no one
needs to read the Talmud to understand the significance of Torah
study in Judaism. One can simply attend a Saturday morning service
in a synagogue to witness the grandeur and reverence attributed to
storing, parading, and reading from the Torah. The Torah is revered
in this way because all other Jewish teachings and values are derived
from it; all subsequent sources of Jewish wisdom and practice descend
from the Torah itself, comprising the "garden around the Torah." In
fact, when we refer to Torah study, we are not referring to the Five
Books of Moses alone, but to all the connective literature and teachings that the Torah has inspired. *Torah study* is therefore a broad term

referring to Jewish learning that is associated with the Torah and the Hebrew Bible, as well as Jewish values and practice.

Torah Study as a Spiritual Practice

But might Torah study be a spiritual practice in and of itself? In other words, is there something about the process of Torah study that offers us spiritual benefits? Yes. Learning Torah is not merely recounting names, places, and laws. According to educational psychologist Benjamin Bloom's famous taxonomy of the six domains of learning, Torah study dwells among the highest, including analysis, synthesis, and evaluation. This is not a result of the fact that we study or even what we study, but the manner in which we study—the Jewish approach to how we study is itself the means by which our intellect grows and our spirits are moved. We can gain access to the spirit by how we focus our intellect.

There are three primary principles that distinguish how Torah is studied so that the process confers spiritual benefits.

1. We Don't Have to Take It Literally

The Torah is an epic poem and, because it is poetic, the words and verses are subject to infinite levels of understanding and interpretation. For example, the Torah says that the world was created in just seven days. But the tradition does not rest with that literal reading. The Midrash and the medieval commentators are all quick to render the seven days figuratively, claiming that a day in God's eyes is equivalent to millennia.[2] The Torah says in Exodus (chap. 21) that a person should be exacted justice "an eye for an eye, a tooth for a tooth ..." but the rabbis of the Talmud interpret the verse to mean that the perpetrator should pay money for restitution.[3] In Deuteronomy (chap. 21), the Torah says that a disobedient boy who is gluttonous and drinks too much wine should be stoned to death, but the rabbis of the Talmud say that there never was such a case and that it was only hypothetical.[4]

There are countless laws and ideas in the Torah that are reduced, expanded, and overturned through the process of interpretation. The stark and naked truth is that Judaism does not follow the Torah. Judaism follows the path of rabbinic interpretation that continues to evolve throughout the centuries. Some say that Jews are the "People of the Book" when, in fact, Jews are the People of the *Books*; Jews are the people of commentary and interpretation.

What does this mean for us both intellectually and spiritually? It means that we learn in life, as we do in study, that A does not necessarily equal A. A can equal B, or C, or any number of things. Just as a verse or a word can simultaneously mean two things that are diametrically opposed to each other, so can other things in life (e.g., a person can be both a sinner and a saint simultaneously, a man can have feminine qualities and vice versa). Acknowledging that both interpretations descend from the same text or apply to the same thing is literally mind opening, sensitizing us to the depths of truth. Here, we learn that the truth is never black or white, but is layered in a manifold spectrum of colors. This is a profound spiritual lesson about life that is built into how we study.

2. What We Study Is Relevant to Us Today

When we read the Torah, we do not read it as a book of history. The stories did not happen thousands of years ago to ancient strangers— they are happening now. The Torah's themes of interpersonal dynamics, familial relationships, and the role of God and religion in our lives are all human issues that are as real today as ever. The flood of Noah did not happen thousands of years ago; it is happening now and if we do not know that, we are drowning. The escape from Pharaoh and slavery did not happen thousands of years ago; it is happening now. If we do not know that, we are still in bondage. We study as if it applies to us now because it is truly happening now. Maybe it is not literally true that it is happening now, but figuratively it is.

Making what we study spiritually, emotionally, and psychologically relevant to our own lives deepens our spiritual connection by personalizing what we learn. And when we personalize what we learn, we awaken to its application all around us, continuously inspiring new questions, insights, and opportunities for growth.

The truth is, when we personalize the Torah to our own experience, we make it our own. This is how we are uniquely involved in the continuous creation of Torah through our own interpretation. We develop our own Torah, which is both permitted and expected in Judaism. We, today, are just as empowered to create our own Torah, and teach our Torah to others, as the early rabbinic sages were. As one eighteenth-century master put it:

> [The Sages] see the root of everything written in the Torah in its true state, empowering them to interpret. The wholeness of the written Torah is thus dependent upon the oral Torah [i.e., the Talmud and the Midrash]....
>
> This is true of each generation and its interpreters. They make the Torah complete. Torah is interpreted in each generation according to what that generation needs. God enlightens the eyes of each generation's sages [to interpret] His Holy Torah in accord with the soul-root of that generation. One who denies this is like one who denies Torah, God forbid.[5]

As students of Torah we encounter flashes of wisdom and insight, elevating us to a sagely level, even if just for a moment. In that moment, a genuine, divine truth has been revealed to us through our interpretation, and we are encouraged to hold that truth and transmit it to others.

3. The Sacred and the Holy Are Real

No matter what any of us believes about the Torah, whether it was directly handed from God to Moses or whether it was written by groups of people over several generations, the Torah is holy. We revere the Torah, we kiss it, we sing about it, and we glorify it. By recognizing the holiness of the Torah, we discern the contrast between what is holy and what is unholy and corrupted. We need this distinction in our lives because we soon discover that there is a substantial disparity between what is holy and what is not holy in the world. The world and humanity do not live up to what they ought to be. There is a tragic gap between the ideal and the real. The ideal is that there is peace, but the reality is that there is war; the ideal is that no one goes hungry, but the reality is that far too many go hungry; the ideal is that the world is just and fair to all, but the reality is that it is unjust and unfair. Through Torah study we raise our consciousness to identify this gap, and by identifying it we better direct our hopes, our prayers, and our aims as a species. Indeed, the mere presence of Torah as a symbol of holiness in our lives encourages us to search for creative solutions and to dream of what is possible.

Study and AA

Now that we have unpacked the spiritual components of Torah study, how does it align with the Steps of AA? Torah study is inherently linked to the same underlying concepts established in Steps 1 and 2. In Step 1, we affirm that we are powerless and that our lives have become unmanageable. That is, we *honestly* acknowledge that life is hard. There is a piece of ourself that cannot cope with life the way we are living. Even though we have denied it over and over, we are not in control of our life and on our own we will ruin it through addiction.

Once we have stopped denying our powerlessness over life, Step 2 is there to provide the response. In other words, in Step 1 we acknowledge that we are lacking power and Step 2 claims that there is a power greater than ourself that can supply the power we lack; lest we fall into despair from our honest reckoning of powerlessness, Step 2 provides hope.

Still, Step 2 and the notion of a power greater than ourself pose one of the most severe challenges to anyone encountering AA. What, after all, is a power greater than ourself? Is it God? What if I do not know what God is? What if I am unsure whether or not I believe in

God? What if I think religion is nonsense? The common response to these questions in the rooms of AA is that, to begin with, anything can be our greater power. For example, the group or fellowship of AA can be our greater power. Our sponsor can be our greater power. It is often said: "It doesn't matter what the greater power is, as long as it's not you."

Here, Judaism does one better than AA. First of all, Judaism agrees that as far as the concept of God is concerned, there is no right or wrong answer. But how we proceed to define that concept and establish a sense of a greater power in our lives is through Torah study. Once we begin Torah study, we are immediately thrust into a sense of reverence for the history of the Torah, the layers of scholarship and wisdom attached to the Torah, and the communal conversation prompted by the Torah that has gone on for thousands of years. Learning and rabbinic scholarship and wisdom become a power greater than ourself that has the potential to unlock a spiritual connection to God.

In this way, by accepting that Torah study has something to offer us, something to teach us, we inherently become willing and teachable. We inherently become reverent—if not reverent to the text itself, then to the process of study. We inherently understand that something holy and meaningful is happening in our learning, as we are becoming more thoughtful and insightful. This is what is supposed to happen in Step 1 and Step 2.

Moreover, in AA, we are given a book to study—*The Big Book of Alcoholics Anonymous.* As with Torah study, we are supposed to find resonances and relevance to our own lives in the *Big Book.* Even though it was written long ago, it is relevant to us. And just as with Torah study, by finding our own experiences and self in it, we make it our own. We begin to develop our own "AA Torah," which we will one day pass down to those we serve as sponsors.

Getting a sponsor, by the way—which should happen at the outset of AA involvement—is a critical feature of recovery so that there is someone to take us through the Steps in the book. This is also aligned with Jewish spirituality. The Mishnah proclaims: "Select a teacher for yourself."[6] Maimonides comments on this teaching that we should pick a teacher even if he is less educated than we are. The point here is that we need someone with experience who can help sharpen our questions, sharpen our thinking, and hold us accountable. We need to humble ourself and be honest with someone about our spiritual process and what we are learning. Ultimately, we are only able to incorporate our learning into our being by having it reflected back to us by another human being. As the Hasidic master Rabbi Jacob Yitzchak put it: "The way cannot be learned out of a book, or from hearsay, but only communicated from person to person."[7] In many ways, this is what sponsorship is all about in AA—we need trusted counsel with whom we can honestly discuss our challenges in life and share our common hope.

Chapter 7

Prayer— *Tefilah*

Out of the depth we cry for help. We believe that we are able to overcome ulterior motives, since otherwise no good would be done, and no love would be possible. Yet to attain purity of heart we are in need of divine help. This is why we pray: "Purify our hearts so that we may serve You honestly" (the Sabbath liturgy).[1]

—Abraham Joshua Heschel, *God in Search of Man*

What is it that we fear most? Is it that we are afraid of losing our sense of self? Is it that we are afraid of dying? Our greatest fear is losing our sense of connection. We fear aimlessly floating in the abyss entirely and utterly alone. In a way, utter loneliness and disconnection are a sort of death, since living is essentially connection. As spiritual leader and author Rabbi Harold Schulweis said, "It is not that I am afraid of dying, it is that I am afraid of never having truly lived."[2] And what is truly living if it is not genuinely engaging our authentic self with others, with the world, and with God? When we strip down to the core of our being beneath flesh and mind, when we are left with nothing but existence itself and the angst that often accompanies it, we find ourself alone in prayer.

Real prayer is not language or speech. Real prayer cannot be rote. Prayer is a stretching and reaching out of the spirit to connect in love. Simply put, there are just some experiences that are so powerful, so awe-inspiring, that we cannot bear them alone. We feel it in the awesomeness of becoming a parent. Exhilaration, a deep gratitude, and a humbling fear accompany that experience. We also feel it when we experience loss or perhaps hit our bottom, which alcoholics and addicts know all too well. We experience utter powerlessness, devastating anguish, and also a humbling fear. So, too, in this state of being, we yearn to reach out and connect from our loneliness. The compulsion to connect is both the need to pray and prayer itself. The act of praying is putting form and expression to the urge that is already inside.

We do not, however, have to experience such earth-shattering highs or lows to have the impulse to connect. We actually experience it all the time, because life as a human being is inherently awe-inspiring. Unfortunately, we are all experts at denying it. We are very talented at distracting ourselves with the social drama and the politics of the day. Also, in our technologically oriented world, we are especially adept at distracting ourselves with the "stuff" we have: our cars, computers, smartphones, tablets, and televisions. The mind loves to work and figure out the puzzles of our contemporary world, and it is happy to be given more and more to occupy it. Meanwhile, the soul grows stagnant and begins to decay, as it is denied its need for expression and connection.

Prayer in this light is a striving forth for connection. Yet prayer is also a self-reflective act. While we reach out, we look back at ourself; we seek a witness to affirm our living experience, while we witness it ourself. Prayer, therefore, is not merely begging and requesting as the English implies. In Hebrew, prayer is *tefilah*, from the word *lehit'palel*. *Lehit'palel* is a reflexive verb, literally meaning to judge or act as witness to ourself. By striving forth to connect with another, while simultaneously being aware of our own experience, the invisible mental and emotional walls that separate us begin to topple. We are then able to see ourself alive in our most natural and vulnerable state; we see ourself through God's eyes.

Connecting I, You, and Us

To whom or to what do we strive to connect? What connection or relationship satisfies our spiritual need? There are three primary relationships to which we seek to connect. First, we strive to gain a better sense of self. We need a sense of *I* in order to be whole in the world. As Hillel famously said, "If I am not for myself, who will be for me?"[3] Traditionally, the first thing Judaism asks us to do in the morning upon waking, the first expression we make at the start of life each day, is to say: "*Modeh Ani* ... Thank You, God, for restoring my soul to me with compassion and great trust." In other words, we say, "Thank you for giving me what is uniquely me." We need to say this because each day we need to know that at our very first moment of consciousness we are the most beautiful being on earth. All of us are human beings, children of the Source of all Life, God's greatest accomplishment. Just think of how awesome it is to be a human, all the things we do with our minds and our hands and our hearts. We have infinite value and we must know it. If we do not affirm our infinite worth and inherent divinity every single day, we are left unwhole.

Fulfilling our *Tikkun*

The great teachers of Jewish mysticism taught that each day, when we wake up, we rise again to our own unique *tikkun*, our own individual purpose in the world, in partnership with the Divine. Each of us has our own unique *tikkun* to fulfill, which we reengage each day. The letters in the word *tikkun* can actually be rearranged to spell *tinok*, which means child or baby. From this we can learn that each day when we wake up it is as if we are born again as children to our unique potential and purpose. In other words, that same energy that was in the world when we came into being is there again each day, and we have the innate power to utilize it and heal ourself and the world.

Second, we strive to connect with You. That is the You with a capital *Y*—God. We will not be whole and feel connected with just a sense of *I*. We need a sense of You for the sake of humility in the world. Hillel said: "If I am not for myself, who will be for me?" but then immediately followed with this question: "But if I am only for myself, what am I?" We need the perspective of God to whom we can defer, to revere, honor. We need God to ask forgiveness and confess our sins. We need a You to thank for all we have been given. We need a You to express our requests and needs for ourself and for others.

Reaching Out to God

Having a sense of You, a sense of God, however, does not mean that we are constrained or pressed beneath God's thumb, so to speak. We can think and believe freely in Judaism, and still have coherence in how we behave. In our behavior, we conform to standards because there are certain things that we must do or just should not do. And that is how we forge community and live civilly. We can sit and make community happen, for example, not because we all agree and have the same faith, believing the same thing, but because we all take the same day off—Shabbat. We observe the same holidays, we have the same eating customs, we marry the same way, we bury loved ones and mourn the same way, we all learn the same language (Hebrew), and we are all held to the same moral standards. The idea that we have coherent behavior comes from that sense of You—of Other. It gives us a sense of commandedness and belonging that humbles us, yet also empowers us to do the right thing.

And finally, the third point of connection we endeavor to establish is the relationship with community—our place of belonging—a connection of Us. First, we acknowledge the infinite value and beauty of the self. Second, we acknowledge the awe and grandeur of You—a power greater than ourself. We are grateful for the gift of these perspectives, and with our gifts and human freedoms, we acknowledge that we also must act responsibly with these freedoms. And so we turn to community.

Forging a Community

We ask, What kind of community shall we have? What kind of schools should educate our children? What kind of neighborhoods should we build? What kind of house of worship shall we build together? Will we be welcoming and respectful? Will we be generous with our time and money? After all, we are inseparable, so what makes us, us? In this way, prayer reminds us of our own responsibility and role in partnering to improve the world. Heschel points out that beyond the awe of the Divine, the purpose of prayer is not to beg God for salvation, but to inspire us to look out to our communities to make the world a better and more just place: "Prayer may not save us, but prayer may make us worthy of being saved."[4]

The triad of self and God cannot be complete without acknowledging the interconnectedness that we have with all others on earth. We simply cannot be spiritually free ourself if we see others enslaved; we cannot be spiritually sated when we see others go hungry; we cannot be spiritually at home when we see others homeless; and we cannot be at peace when violence is present. We are not truly at rest when we stand idly by; to connect we must supply connection.

Prayer, therefore, enables us to gain a greater sense of *I*, *You*, and *Us*, or Self, God, and Community. Prayer is also something we need every day because we need to remind ourself of the connections that affirm our existence and self-worth every day. Indeed, this is self-healing.

Prayer and AA

It is no secret that prayer and meditation are critical components of the 12 Steps. Steps 3, 6, 7, and 11 are all related to a form of prayerfulness. In fact, Steps 3 and 7 have specific prayers associated with them from the *Big Book*. Moreover, AA meetings usually begin in prayer (often the Serenity Prayer) and end in prayer. Why is that? What is it about the spiritual striving for connection and self-reflection that addresses our character and helps us stop drinking and using?

As human beings we all have character defects. Part of the 12 Steps is for alcoholics and addicts to identify their character defects. Most of us share some of the same ones. The temptations that we experience, which usually result in bad or destructive behavior, often stem from these character defects. Prayer is a proven activity that helps neutralize these temptations, giving us greater awareness of our character defects and the power we have over them.

In Step 3, for example, when we agree to turn over our will and our lives to God, as we understand the Divine, the temptation is to give in to our own self-will. Our self-will can run riot and manifest in hundreds of forms. Here, self-will is synonymous with the *yetzer ha-ra*, meaning that we will give in to our selfishness, denying how it might affect others or even ourself in the long run. The Step 3 Prayer, as it appears in the *Big Book*, emphasizes striving to align our will with God's. It is to acknowledge and affirm the discomfort we may feel in that moment, but to recognize that resorting to self-centered, immediate relief and pleasure (such as drinking, using, overeating, sex, or even throwing a tantrum) is neither a wise nor a good course. Instead, we connect to the lens of the greater "You" to guide us in that moment to be better connected to ourself and others.

Steps 6 and 7 are process prayers. They come immediately after Step 5, which is after we have opened up to our sponsor about our resentments and have identified our character defects. When we are open and vulnerable like that, we are left with a choice. The choice is whether or not we are willing and humble enough to accept those as our defects and commit to working on letting them go. The temptation is to become stubborn and prideful, to deny our shortcomings and resist doing the work necessary to heal. The Step 7 Prayer again returns to the lens of the greater "You" so that we can see that we have the strength to be willing and humble to do our part in connecting to others.

Step 11 calls on us to maintain the ongoing practice of prayer and meditation in our lives. There we continuously tap into the connection we need with ourself, God, and community. Through Step 11, we integrate a life of prayer and self-reflection, consistently being aware of what and who we are, and what we are doing. The temptation is to complete the prior Steps and to wander aimlessly, lying to ourself that we have spiritually graduated. In Step 11, we remind ourself that alcoholism and addiction are "isms," meaning that they continue to happen. We require a perspective outside of ourself—God and community—that provides us with feedback so that we can be the potential human being we are intended to be. Step 11 relieves us from living a self-conscious life, and guides us to living a God-conscious life. As prominent religious leader Rabbi Morris Adler once put it: "Our prayers are not answered when we are given what we ask, but when we are challenged to be what we can be."[5]

Chapter 8

Repentance— *Teshuvah*

When all these things befall you—the blessing and the curse that I have set before you—and you take them to heart ... and you return [*teshuvah*] to the Lord your God, and you and your children heed this command with all your heart and soul, just as I enjoin upon you this day, then the Lord your God will restore your fortunes and take you back in love ... Then the Lord your God will circumcise your heart and the hearts of your offspring to love the Lord with all your heart and soul, in order that you may live. (Deuteronomy 30:1–6)

If we could, what would we change about our character? Is there something about ourself we would change? Are we too impatient? Do we get angry too quickly? Procrastinate too much? How about changing something we did? In other words, if we could change something we did in the past, what would we change?

There are those who believe that nothing ever truly changes. They believe that life is a circle, merely repeating itself in different forms. They believe that no one changes and that history is doomed to repeat itself. That, however, is not the spirituality of Judaism. History is not doomed to repeat itself, neither in our own personal lives nor as a species. Rather than a circle, Judaism claims that life spirals upward, ever closer to the Divine, ever improving and moving toward more wholeness and goodness. We are not degenerating, falling further away from the holiness of the past or from God's revelation at Sinai; rather, we are closer to the Divine than ever before. Judaism is a spirituality of optimism and the mechanism by which this spiritual progression advances is *teshuvah*, or repentance.

The Process of Spiritual Transformation

Teshuvah, from the verb root meaning "to return," is the process by which spiritual transformation or change happens. This kind of change can occur in our own character, and when we change our character, we change our behavior and can repair things we have done in the past. That is, we cannot change what was actually done, but we can change the meaning of the past by changing the present. We may have come up short in the past, but if, in the end, we come clean and emerge on top of life, the past becomes a stepping-stone to success, rather than ending in failure. It must be this way, after all: If we were unable to change and our character was hopelessly trapped by its early development and past deeds, what point would there be to the future? As the Hasidic master Rabbi Nachman of Breslov rhetorically asked: "If we are not better tomorrow than we are today, then why have tomorrow?"[1]

So critical is *teshuvah*—the process by which we can change and improve ourself and our past—that the rabbinic sages teach that *teshuvah* was a spiritual principle built into the natural structure of the universe, before God began creating the physical world.[2] And even though *teshuvah* is infrequently mentioned in the Hebrew Bible, the rabbinic tradition strongly embraces it, claiming: "Great is *teshuvah* for it brings healing to the whole world, and an individual who repents is forgiven and the whole world is forgiven."[3] Moreover, the entire High Holiday season, the most sacred days of the Jewish calendar (from Rosh Hashanah through Yom Kippur), is entirely dedicated to *teshuvah*, called *Aseret Yemei Teshuvah*, the Ten Days of *Teshuvah*.

The first thing to know about *teshuvah* is that it is an action, not a thought or feeling. Sure, we could think we would like to change or be sorry for past deeds, but until we actually do something about it, we have not done *teshuvah*. Thinking we are sorry and doing something about feeling sorry have inherently different spiritual values. Through the act itself of making amends or doing something differently, we see the change of mind manifest in the world, which has much greater impact.

First Comes the Awakening

Even though *teshuvah* is ultimately completed in the form of deed, it functionally begins with a realization or an awakening. A person arrives, either suddenly or gradually, at a turning point in life of severe discomfort. A gnawing unease and anxiety takes hold, disturbing us out of the present. And whether or not we have faith in God, we are pressed to change—life can no longer move forward in the direction we have taken. We see that we are flawed and that if we are going to find peace, something must be done. Once we have awakened to this realization, we can either choose to live freely by making an effort to change and amend our wrongdoings, or we can choose to live in the numbing illusion of our lie. The lie holds that what we have done and who we are do not matter; the lie holds that it is possible to live a divided, disingenuous life.

As we continue to reflect on our past deeds and approaches to life—if we're engaging in an honest and thorough reflection—we begin to see our part in the discomfort that we feel. We begin to see how the choices we made contributed to our pain and, as we dig deeper, we may even recognize the false assumptions we had about others or the world that led to our behavior. Perhaps we assumed people knew how we felt and could read our minds; perhaps we assumed the worst, rather than giving others the benefit of the doubt; or perhaps we were selfish in only considering our own feelings and not those of others. Such assumptions, whether conscious or subconscious, usually lead to misunderstanding, fear, resentment, and anger. When we see our own part and take responsibility for it, we turn toward our higher selves and toward our greater power.

Teshuvah and Steps 4 and 5

Step 4 of AA mirrors this process of *teshuvah*. In Step 4 we take a moral inventory of ourself. We are supposed to look at people, institutions, systems, and even ideas that we resent. Once we identify our resentments, we then look at ourself and take responsibility for ways in which we have contributed to those situations—the good and the bad. The temptation is to ignore relationships for which we hold resentments and to deny the part we have played in them. Of course, we know that, as adults, no relationship is entirely one-sided and that there is always give-and-take. But we may be afraid to face our own selfishness, the lies we have told, the truths we have omitted, the grudges we have borne. Step 4, which should be done with a sponsor, takes courage and ruthless honesty. The truth is that everyone has resentments, and *teshuvah* invites us to address the bitterness that resides within us and clear the air.

The next stage of *teshuvah* is to confess our wrongdoing. *Teshuvah* is more than regret and a personal vow to ourself not to repeat the behavior. We must right past wrongs, and confessing them aloud to another is how we begin to become accountable. Step 5 parallels this part of the process. It is when we tell our story of wrongdoing, no matter how embarrassing, in a nonjudgmental, safe setting with our sponsor. Confessing to God is also good, but we need another human being in the here and now to be the receptacle for our story. By telling another person, hearing ourself tell the story aloud, and having it reflected back to us by another, we take a greater step toward honesty and integrity. Our sponsor can also then use some of that information to help guide us through the next steps of the process of *teshuvah*.

The *Big Book* beautifully describes the spiritual experience of this confession in Step 5. Here it portrays a great sense of relief that overwhelms us because we have let go of the sin and the lie that have imprisoned our spirit, preventing us from connecting with the world:

> We pocket our pride and go to it, illuminating every twist of character, every dark cranny of the past. Once we have taken this step, withholding nothing, we are delighted. We can look the world in the eye. We can be alone at perfect peace and ease. Our fears fall from us. We begin to feel the nearness of our Creator. We may have had certain spiritual beliefs, but now we begin to have a spiritual experience. The feeling that the drink problem has disappeared will often come strongly. We feel we are on the Broad Highway, walking hand in hand with the Spirit of the Universe.[4]

Judaism also speaks of the power of confession during *teshuvah*. Rabbi Abraham Isaac Kook, the first chief rabbi of the modern State of Israel, wrote extensively about *teshuvah* and the transcendent spiritual experience that accompanies it. Undoubtedly, the spiritual liberation and cleansing that come from facing and admitting our sins that Kook describes in the following passage are very similar to the selection from the *Big Book* above:

> There is *teshuvah* corresponding to a specific sin as well as to many sins. Man places his sin "before his face" and is caught in the snare of his sin. His soul climbs and ascends till he is completely freed of bondage to sin; he senses within himself the sacred freedom, so pleasant to his weary soul, and

is progressively cured. And the radiant lights of the sun of mercy, transcendental mercy, cast their rays upon him and he becomes joyful, he becomes filled with inner pleasure and delight, though simultaneously enduring a broken heart as well as a humbled and contrite soul—for he senses within himself that this very feeling, appropriate to him according to his present state, increases his spiritual pleasure and aids him toward true perfection. He constantly senses that he is coming ever closer to the source of life, to the Living God from Whom he was but a short while ago so remote. His yearning soul remembers with a joyful heart its inner affliction and anguish and it is overwhelmed with feelings of thankfulness; with praise and song it lifts its voice....[5]

After we complete Step 5, we move into a place of prayerfulness, humbly seeking to rid ourself of the defects that separate our will from God's and from connecting with others. The process of *teshuvah* is layered with prayerful opportunities, each with the intent to see others and ourself through the eyes of God. Prayer during *teshuvah* provides us with focus and encouragement to do what we know is right.

Teshuvah and Steps 8 and 9

For *teshuvah* to be complete, we must go to those we have hurt and wronged. We must apologize, pledge to never repeat the same offense, and offer to make amends in any way we can. If there is money owed, it should be repaid. If something was stolen, it must be returned. And if there is no concrete form of repayment to be made, a sincere apology is in order. The Jewish tradition adds a helpful guideline, teaching us that we need only apologize up to three times. Anything beyond that is unnecessary and it is then up to the wronged party to offer forgiveness on her own.

Members of AA will quickly identify this stage of *teshuvah* as Steps 8 and 9. In Step 8, we identify the people we have wronged and consider the ways in which we can make amends to them. In Step 9, we go and actually make our amends. It is important to note that we only confess our transgressions and make amends in a way that would not cause more harm. We do not need to say everything we think simply because it makes us feel better. We are to apologize, offer to make amends, and then just listen. If someone is deceased or we cannot locate him, we must remain willing to make such amends, if only in our prayers.

Teshuvah: An Everyday Occurrence

As long as we are human beings, we will be imperfect and make mistakes; errors are simply part of the game, part of life's rigorous path. Some mistakes will be more dramatic than others and in need of more dramatic amends. Whether mistakes are big or small, however, there will certainly be resentments. At times, we will react harshly to those resentments. Therefore, *teshuvah* is something we engage in every day. Every day, we build Step 10 into our daily routine, taking regular inventory of what we resented, when we were dishonest, when we were selfish, and what we were afraid of. If any of these feelings and experiences come up for us, we must tell someone and use it as an opportunity to address the problem as soon as possible.

Interestingly, in Judaism, *teshuvah* is not an annual event at the High Holidays, but a daily one. We ask God to forgive us every single day in our prayer, referring to God as the "One who wants *teshuvah*." And since God wants *teshuvah* every day, we can assume that God expects us to make mistakes every day. We have daily confessionals in our prayers. These are not like the confessionals and absolutions of Catholicism. Instead, we confess directly to God and to the one we have wronged.

The process of *teshuvah* is not easy. It takes a great deal of courage to both admit our imperfections and flaws, and then to face them with those we have wronged. It demands a collapse of pride and often results in a change to a new identity. But it can and has been done time and again. It has been done by anyone who has worked the AA Steps. It is the process that makes second chances (sometimes third, fourth, and fifth) possible. It allows us to either start our lives over, even at late stages in life, or reenter previous lives, with our family and community. Recognizing the magnitude of *teshuvah*, the Talmud stands in awe of those who sincerely go through its process, declaring: "Even the most righteous among us cannot stand in the place where one who has done *teshuvah* stands."[6]

Chapter 9

Service— *Tikkun*

The final goal of wisdom is to turn to God and to do good works. (B. Talmud, *Menachot* 110a)

The great mystic, Isaac Luria, had a vision of time before time. In the beginning, he taught, there was no space, no time, no matter—only the energy and presence of God. But God felt divided and detached. God had the impulse to change, to grow, to create. In a way, God needed a helpmate.

Since there was only God, for God to create, God had to take a piece of God's self and transform it into matter and into the universe. God formed a vessel out of God's own self to house the universe. This vessel would carry God's energy toward unification and wholeness. Tragically, however, when God poured the divine energy into the vessel, the energy was too overwhelming and bright to be contained. The vessel shattered into pieces. Each shard scattered, yet remained attached to the emanation of energy and light that it touched.

Thus, according to Jewish mystical cosmology, the universe has been fundamentally broken since its very beginning. Teachers and later mystics have elaborated on the vision of the world as a broken cosmos—divinely shattered vessels attached to light—to include each part of the universe, including us. In other words, not only is the whole universe broken and divided, but so is each of us—broken shards affixed to and wrapped in light.

Hearkening back to an earlier rabbinic concept—*tikkun olam* (literally, "fixing the world")—which generally signified promoting the welfare of the community,[1] Luria applied his concept of God and the universe. He claimed that our purpose is to literally fix the world by putting the shattered vessel back together. His concept, however, was mostly introspective. Luria taught that God manifests in the world through spiritual emanations called *sefirot*, which also have personality traits (e.g., compassion). By meditating on each of these *sefirot* and their unification, we can help heal our shattered world. In 1964, the chief rabbi of Israel, Abraham Isaac Kook, expanded on Luria's concept when he wrote that *tikkun olam* must not be a process that "flies about solely in the spiritual ether," but must equitably bring together physical, social, and spiritual concerns.[2]

Healing the World's Brokenness

Tikkun olam, or simply *tikkun*, is ultimately the beautiful idea that we—as human beings—are a critical part of the unfolding of God's creation and will. When we balance ourselves through spiritual practice and then align our spiritual clarity with how we relate to others and the world, we can help heal the world's brokenness. We embody *tikkun* in our actions of service, when we recognize the pain and brokenness in others, connect ourselves to them, and then serve their needs so that they can become whole. Sometimes our service comes in the form of providing for physical needs, such as food, clothing, shelter, or money. Sometimes our service is in the form of social or political needs, such as advocacy, protest, or education. And sometimes our service is in the form of responding to spiritual and emotional needs, such as listening, praying, sympathizing, and counseling.

We might ask, How is an alcoholic or an addict—a drunk or a junkie—fit to do any sort of healing and service for others? Drunks and junkies cannot even take care of themselves, right? Wrong. While it is true that in early recovery from alcohol and drugs, alcoholics and addicts need quite a bit of healing themselves, once they have started on the road to health and wholeness, working the Steps and living in honesty, alcoholics and addicts excel in acts of service. Just within AA alone, many are deeply involved in service, sponsoring other alcoholics and addicts, raising money for and helping hospitals and institutions, and running AA meetings. And that is just in AA alone, which does not include the general work and service they are contributing beyond AA.

Unfortunately, to begin recovery, most alcoholics and addicts have experienced tremendous loss. Through our addiction, we have lost jobs, families, and homes. Many of us have been put in prison and have gone through financial collapse. These things happened not because we wanted them to, but because we could not help ourselves and we could not stop them from happening. During the process, our hearts were broken. People we loved abandoned us, all we cared about slipped away, and our identity was shattered. We became what we feared. We despised ourself.

Broken Open

Considering the mystical conception of a world created broken, with broken people, it is no wonder such terrible things happen. That is simply the way the world was formed. But our purpose is to find healing for ourselves and provide healing for others. Therefore, there is something we might learn from heartbreak. Heartbreak does not, and for Judaism, must not, end in tragedy. In fact, heartbreak can lead to more openness, capaciousness, and power. The great sociologist and educator Parker Palmer describes this point succinctly:

There are at least two ways to picture a broken heart, using *heart* in its original meaning not merely as the seat of the emotions but as the core of our sense of self. The conventional image, of course, is that of a heart broken by unbearable tension into a thousand shards—shards that sometimes become shrapnel aimed at the source of our pain. Every day, untold numbers of people try to "pick up the pieces," some of them taking grim satisfaction in the way the heart's explosion has injured their enemies. Here the broken heart is an unresolved wound that we too often inflict on others.

But there is another way to visualize what a broken heart might mean. Imagine that small, clenched fist of a heart "broken open" into largeness of life, into greater capacity to hold one's own and the world's pain and joy. This, too, happens every day. Who among us has not seen evidence, in our own or other people's lives, that compassion and grace can be the fruits of great suffering? Here heartbreak becomes a source of healing, enlarging our empathy and extending our ability to reach out.[3]

According to Palmer's second description of heartbreak, we can begin to see the potential good that can emerge from this. And we are witnesses to it all the time. We see mothers who lose their children to drunk driving later become powerful advocates for awareness, safety, and social change. We see survivors of cancer and other diseases who become the greatest sources of inspiration and strength to others. We see the spiritually and emotionally downtrodden and depressed arise to become great agents of hope (Palmer himself being one of them). Heartbreak occurs time and again throughout history, and out of heartbreak some of our greatest political leaders, artists, and spiritual masters have grown. They include President Abraham Lincoln, British Prime Minister Winston Churchill, philosopher William James, composer Wolfgang Amadeus Mozart, and author Mark Twain (to name just a few). We also find many great Jewish leaders who were broken and even suicidal, including biblical figures, such as Moses, Elijah the Prophet, Jonah the Prophet, and King David, as well as the rabbinic greats Maimonides and Nachman of Breslov.

Of course, no one would ever wish brokenness or heartbreak on anyone because of the suffering involved, but heartbreak has the potential to motivate us to awaken our sense of gratitude and inspire goodness. The Hebrew Bible often speaks of "circumcising the heart" as a metaphor for making us less callous and more empathetic toward others.[4] What Judaism acknowledges in the Hebrew Bible, as well as through Luria's conception of a broken world, is that every human being experiences brokenness and heartbreak in some form or another. The question is what we do about it. The following Hasidic story speaks of how, through brokenness and heartbreak, we can elevate ourself:

> A disciple asks the rebbe: "Why does the Torah tell us to 'place these words *upon* your hearts' (Deut. 11:18)? Why does it not tell us to place these holy words *in* our hearts?" The rebbe answers: "It is because as we are, our hearts are closed, and we cannot place the holy words in our hearts. So we place them on top of our hearts. And there they stay until one day, the heart breaks and the words fall in."[5]

The rabbinic tradition quickly responded to the question of what to do with brokenness and a broken heart. The greatest tragedy in Jewish history is traditionally understood to be the destruction of the Second Temple in 70 CE. This is when the Romans sacked and burned the center of Jewish life in Jerusalem. Not only did they destroy the Holy Temple itself, but they also destroyed all that was attached to it, including the Jewish court of law (the *Sanhedrin*), the marketplace beside it, and the heart of Jewish living and tradition. There were many questions as to how Judaism would survive without the Temple as the seat of worship. How were Jews to serve God and atone for sins without the Temple and the offering of sacrifices? The sages were quick to respond in the following talmudic passage, which is recited each morning in many traditional circles:

> Once, Rabban Yochanan ben Zakkai was walking with his disciple, Rabbi Yehoshua, near Jerusalem after the destruction of the Temple. Rabbi Yehoshua looked at the Temple ruins and said: "Alas for us! The place that atoned for the sins of the people Israel—the ritual of animal sacrifice—lies in ruins!" Then Rabban Yochanan ben Zakkai spoke to him these words of comfort: "Be not grieved, my son. There is another equally meritorious way of gaining atonement even though the Temple is destroyed. We can still gain atonement through deeds of loving-kindness." For it is written, *Loving-kindness I desire, not sacrifice* (Hosea 6:6).[6]

The passage above teaches two significant lessons. One is the power of acts of loving-kindness. Acts of loving-kindness represent the *tikkun* that we have been discussing. They are acts of service that spring from empathy and warmth without expectation of reward. Such acts of service are themselves, according to Judaism, service to God as much as worship itself. Second, one of the critical reasons to offer sacrifices in the Temple was to atone for sins. Sacrificing a valuable animal reflected the abstract emotional and spiritual process that occurred inside the individual. When an individual saw his precious animal slaughtered and cooked, with smoke rising to the heavens, he believed and experienced the weight of his sins lifted and he could return to life with a clear conscience. Here, we see that doing an act of goodness and healing for another can serve the same function. Many of us know this from our own experience. That is, doing something good for another helps ease the sting of our own guilt and suffering—it lifts our spirits to know we have done something good and healing. American author

Mark Twain put it well when he said: "The best way to cheer yourself up is to cheer up somebody else."

Service and AA

Early in the history of AA, there was a symbol of a triangle surrounded by a circle that represented the three legacies of AA. Outside each of the three sides of the triangle and inside the circle was a word: *Recovery, Unity,* and *Service.* These three words signify the three essential components of AA, paralleling the mental, physical, and spiritual aspects of the disease and its solution. Recovery is linked to our mental obsession; Unity is linked to the AA group body, and the importance of community and fellowship; and Service is linked to the spirituality expressed directly in Step 12: Having had a spiritual awakening as the result of these Steps, we tried to carry this message to alcoholics, and to practice these principles in all our affairs.

Although the triangle and circle symbol stopped being used in the 1990s, due to printing costs and controversy over defending the right to use the symbol, Recovery, Unity, and Service are still prominent principles of AA. Interestingly, regarding the principle of service, the AA founders recognized very early what Judaism has long known about spirituality and healing. They discovered that our own healing must be passed on to others in acts of kindness for spirituality to be entirely realized. Acting in service of others without expectation of reward is fundamentally a spiritual act. We might benefit from service by continuing our own learning and growth, but our intention is to give back to others what we were once given ourself. We were broken and needed help to heal and, now that we are well into our healing, we must transmit it to others.

One of the most poignant experiences of an alcoholic or addict is to walk into our first AA or NA meeting. There we are in a church basement or fellowship hall, totally broken, ashamed, and believing that we are all alone in the world. We are greeted at the door by a stranger—maybe a tattooed ex-con, a businessman, or a housewife.

We are shocked by the diversity. Then we begin to listen to the stories and we realize that no matter how anyone might look, we all share the same basic experience. We are all broken and our worlds are broken. Hopefully, we gain a bit of perspective and begin to understand that healing, that *tikkun*, is possible. However, we are also introduced to the concept of a sponsor, which is someone who will work with us, listen to us, and help us help ourself. At that moment, we are afraid of such an awe-inspiring relationship. Many of us, however, cannot avoid projecting into the future when we have some sobriety behind us. We are aware that we are not ready to be a sponsor ourself at this moment, but we know that someday we will be. We will be helping someone else. It may be hard to imagine, yet we imagine it anyway. It is frightening and exciting. We become aware that, despite our current state of brokenness, we are still worth something. We can help someone else because we know her experience and pain, as we are suffering it now. Even though we have not formally completed Step 12, we have already tasted its impact. In fact, we can start to be of service in smaller ways today, right now.

AA strongly supports the uplift that comes from service by working with newcomers and becoming a sponsor. As the *Big Book* states:

> Practical experience shows that nothing will so much insure immunity from drinking as intensive work with other alcoholics. This is our twelfth suggestion: Carry this message to other alcoholics! You can help when no one else can....
>
> Life will take on new meaning. To watch people recover, to see them help others, to watch loneliness vanish, to see a fellowship grow up about you, to have a host of friends—this is an experience you must not miss.[7]

Spirituality is embodied in acts of connection. The most profound level of connection is in teaching and learning. When approached with genuine intention, teaching and learning are a form of inspirational intimacy. Both the teacher and the student become givers and receivers, weaving their hearts together through their mutual experience, strength, and hope. Martin Buber refers to teaching and learning as a spiritual experience of divine revelation when he writes: "The spark that leaps from him who teaches to him who learns, rekindles a spark of that fire which lifted the mountain of revelation 'to the very heart of heaven.'"[8]

Part III

12 Texts for the 12 Steps

Just as I have watched over them to pluck up and to break down, and to overthrow, to destroy, and bring disaster, so I will watch over them to build up and to plant. (Jeremiah 31:28)

There is a well-known Jewish tale of a man who dreams of a treasure. He sees the treasure in his dream so clearly that he can see exactly where it is located. To the man's delight, the treasure is in a nearby city. So he travels to the exact place where he dreamed the treasure was. Instead of finding treasure, however, he meets a stranger who had a similar dream of a treasure. The stranger saw it just as clearly as the man did and, as luck would have it, the treasure the stranger dreamed of was in a nearby city. So the man follows the stranger's directions to the treasure in the nearby city. Lo and behold, this time he finds the treasure. Where was it? It was back in his own home city, indeed at the steps of his own home all along.

The story teaches that our personal gifts and treasures—all we really need—are with us all along. We may not, however, be able to access it or see it until we change our perspective. In other words, we all have everything we need within ourself, but we may be living lives that prevent us from acknowledging our gifts and utilizing them. We need a change in perspective. Such a change in perspective may mean going to a treatment center. It may require health care. In any case, it will call for us to be willing to learn, change our attitudes, and change our behaviors so that what we need can emerge.

Many of us have avoided this kind of change of perspective because it demands a shift in our spirituality. We have avoided this kind of change because it means facing a part of ourself with which we are uncomfortable. Most of all, we have avoided this kind of change because either we did not know how to change or we were afraid to change.

The Steps of AA are intended to help us make the changes necessary so that we can rid our lives of addiction and discover the inherent treasure already within us. They primarily involve deep reflection, uncompromising honesty, and willingness to learn and take direction from another. They are guideposts toward positive change. The wisdom of these Steps is also found in Jewish texts and practices. In fact, there are many, many Jewish texts that could supplant the Steps and it is difficult to choose only one to align with each Step.

The following pages offer Jewish texts and reflections that marry the Steps of AA with Jewish concepts and teachers. In the end, the goal of transformation and change for both Judaism and AA is the same. Such an expression is found in the AA "Promises":

If we are painstaking about this phase of our development, we will be amazed before we are halfway through. We are going to know a new freedom and a new happiness. We will not regret the past nor wish to shut the door on it. We will comprehend the word serenity and we will know peace. No matter how far down the scale we have gone, we will see how our experience can benefit others. That feeling of uselessness and self-pity will disappear. We will lose interest in selfish things and gain interest in our fellows. Self-seeking will slip away. Our whole attitude and outlook upon life will change. Fear of people and of economic insecurity will leave us. We will intuitively know how to handle situations which used to baffle us. We will suddenly realize that God is doing for us what we could not do for ourselves.

Are these extravagant promises? We think not. They are being fulfilled among us—sometimes quickly, sometimes slowly. They will always materialize if we work for them.[1]

The thoughts I've drawn from the Jewish tradition seek to provide a framework that bridges the text with the corresponding Step. Then I work to extract the common kernel of truth about recovery and wholeness that they share.

Step 1

We admitted we were powerless over alcohol—that our lives have become unmanageable.

> I call heaven and earth as a witness today: I have put
> before you life and death, blessing and curse. Choose life.
>
> —Deuteronomy 30:19

Why might the Torah find it necessary to make such a statement? Is there someone who might actually choose curse or, God forbid, death? Who is irrational, odd, or perhaps stupid enough to make that choice? Yet we know that the Torah does not make proclamations like this out of the blue. Obviously, many people (including this author) surely and consistently have chosen curse over blessing, death over life.

Let us consider what choosing curse over blessing or death over life might be. It is to allow the insanity to win out. It is to allow ourself to choose alcohol or drugs over the people we love, including ourself. We are all—without exception—given the message that there is someone who cares, whether it is a family member, a friend, a teacher, or a sponsor and, yet, knowing what we know, we continue to choose suffering over serenity, the dark over the light.

Judaism is not for fools. The Torah here recognizes the tempting traps of the mind and spirit. However, it declares one immutable truth: We can choose. We can choose our perspective. The past is the past and it may be filled with everything from treachery to nonsense, but today—today, we get to choose blessing. Today, we can choose life and the past and the future do not matter. It is simple, but hard. It is hard because the mind's energy has a powerful momentum that can become bound up in our pride. But it is simple because it is merely a matter of the mind and, so, the solution is within our grasp.

Choice—choosing blessing or life—however, assumes a certain level of power. And yet, the first step in AA is to admit that we are powerless. That said, our powerlessness over alcohol and drugs does not mean that we cannot choose whether or not to take that first drink or hit. We can employ the strategy of "No, thank you. I don't drink." We still maintain our power of choice in that moment. After the first drink or hit, we have lost our power. We do not say no to the second.

An AA member once used the following rhetoric to explain: "Would you choose to go to your child's birthday party or have a drink? You'd certainly choose to go to the birthday party, wouldn't you? Now, take that first drink and let me ask you again. Would you choose to go to your child's birthday party or go for your second drink?" As alcoholics, we recognize ourselves in that question. We must admit that powerlessness over alcohol and drugs and unmanageability kicks in once we have that first drink. Judaism adds that we are never completely powerless; we have the power not to choose that first drink or drug. It proclaims that we can choose that, so "Choose life."

Step 2

> In every generation, each person is obligated to see himself as if he had come out from Egypt, as it says, *And you shall explain to your son on that day, "It is because of what the Lord did for me when I went out free from Egypt"* (Exod. 13:8). Not only were our ancestors redeemed by the Holy One blessed be He, but even we were redeemed with them, as it says, *... and us He freed from there, that He might take us and give the land that He had promised on oath to our fathers* (Deut. 6:23).
>
> —Mishnah, *Pesachim* 10:5

> The Exodus from Egypt occurs in every human being, in every era, in every year, and even on every day.
>
> — Rabbi Nachman of Breslov (1772–1810, Ukraine and Russia)

None of us was actually beaten by Egyptian taskmasters, but we act as if we were. None of us survived on slave rations, but we act as if we did. None of us felt the hopeless despair of slavery, but we act as if we did. Are we fools? Of course not!

Even though we did not work the mud pits in Egypt or feel the sting of the taskmaster's whip, we all know what it is to be a slave. To be a slave is to wake up each morning and to feel compelled to do something that we may not want to do and that we know we should not do, but we do it anyway. So it is with drinking—we are slaves to the bottle. We may start in the morning or perhaps we wait until the clock reaches 5:00 p.m., but there we are again, acting according to a will that we despise. The "Beast" (the dark, inner rationalization) says, "Drink. You'll feel better. You'll be able to stop after one. No one will know—it's just you and me." And we obey our master.

The message here, however, is not about the hopeless depravity of our mental slavery. It is about redemption. Redemption is the means by which we "buy back" or "reclaim" something that was originally ours. In this case, we redeem or "take back possession" of our souls, our integrity, and our unique existence. And the only reason we redeem ourself is because we are worth it. God found the Israelites worth it then and God finds each one us of us worth it now. This is why we imagine and act like our enslaved ancestors—to remind us that we are worth redeeming.

In Step 1, we admitted we were powerless—that we lack power. Here in Step 2, we learn that the power we lack lies in the redemptive power of God. In other words, we do not have to be slaves to our addiction if we are willing to allow our cries to be heard and our face to be seen, as our ancestors' were. The pervasive, loving energy that was present at the creation of the world, at our own birth, and at every individual moment of salvation is tethered to our soul, and will give us the strength to pull ourself out of the muck and the mire *if we allow it to*. We must remember and accept that if our ancestors could do it, if our sponsor could do it, then we can do it for ourself, too. In this seed of hope and faith—that it is possible to be redeemed—lies our true power.

Step 3

Made a decision to turn our will and our lives over to the care of God as we understood Him.

A very learned man who had heard of the rabbi [Levi Yitzchak] of Berditchev—one of those who boasted of being enlightened—looked him up in order to debate with him as he was in the habit of doing with others, and refuting his old-fashioned proofs for the truth of his faith. When he entered the tzaddik's [i.e., great, righteous man's] room, he saw him walking up and down, immersed in ecstatic thought. The rabbi took no notice of his visitor. After a time, however, he stopped, gave the learned man a brief glance and said: "But perhaps it is true after all!"

In vain did the learned man try to rally his self-confidence. His knees shook, for the tzaddik was terrible to behold and his simple words were terrible to hear. But now Levi Yitzchak turned to him and calmly addressed him: "My son, the great Torah scholars with whom you have debated wasted their words on you. When you left them you only laughed at what they had said. They could not set God and his kingdom on the table before you, and I cannot do this either. But, my son, only think! Perhaps it is true. Perhaps it is true after all!" The enlightened man made the utmost effort to reply, but the terrible "Perhaps" beat on his ears again and again and broke down his resistance.

—Martin Buber, *Tales from the Hasidim*

The root of the disease of addiction is self-centeredness. This self-centeredness is characterized by obsession and compulsion to control our own reality. In Steps 1 and 2, we begin to accept the fact that we are not in control—not in control of our addiction and not in control of our life. The persistent delusion experienced by alcoholics is the denial of the fact that we are not really in control of much at all, if anything. And so, alcoholics live in the frustrating experience of resisting the reality that confronts them by controlling it through the consumption of alcohol or mind-altering substances. Surrender—true surrender—is accepting reality for what it is and allowing it into one's experience. This means coping with reality: feeling the feelings and thinking the thoughts that come with it.

Alcoholics, by the way, are not alone in their yearning to refuse to accept reality by cloaking the experience. Many people in America today numb their thoughts and feelings through the conspicuous consumption of material goods. There are many "shopaholics" or "spendaholics," yet such terms are met with a smile and perhaps even smugly celebrated, as if a flattened, superficial existence is something worthwhile. The disease of addiction rears its head in any place where human beings place their own need to control above all else.

We know that there are some unfortunates addicted to food, dieting and diet pills, plastic surgery, performance-enhancing supplements and steroids, gambling, video games, criminal behavior, sex, and unhealthy relationships. We might even go so far as to say that addictive behavior can manifest in the adherence to the fundamentals of a particular ideology or religion, whereby the traditions and dogmas of the ideology or religion serve as a means to control and block out genuine experiences and feelings. In a way, each of the aforementioned manifestations of addiction is a way of staying within our own circle of familiarity and comfort.

The point here is to let go. Let go of old ideas and acknowledge a source of information outside our own mind; let go of the habits that confine our life's experience. Perhaps, just perhaps, we have been wrong about life. Perhaps there is something greater than us and we need to concede to it. We have tried and tried to control our experience one way or another, and it is time to unfetter ourself from the chains that bind us, and cede control to a greater power, a greater source of light and peace.

In Step 2, we came to believe that there is something greater than ourself that both binds and is beyond us. To engage Step 3 is to trust that power greater than ourself. It is akin to simply closing our eyes to go to sleep each night. There we are completely vulnerable to the world, yet somehow we trust that we will awaken again and everything will be all right. So it is when we awaken from addiction—we do not know what will happen, we are vulnerable to the world. But we can trust that we will be able to face whatever comes our way and that, somehow, and at some point, everything will be okay.

The Jewish prayer book beautifully expresses the idea of trust in God. Traditionally, it is a custom to recite the following verse both when we rise in the morning and when we retire at night:

> *I place my spirit in His care, when I wake as when I sleep.*
> *God is with me, I shall not fear, body and spirit in His keep.*[1]

Step 4

Made a searching and fearless moral inventory of ourselves.

> Every sin causes a special anxiety on the spirit, which can only be erased by repentance, which transforms the anxiety itself into inner security and courage.
>
> —Abraham Isaac Kook

There is a common misconception that once alcohol and drugs are removed from the life of alcoholics and drug addicts, they are cured. It is easy to see why so many think that. Surely, it would seem that all the problems were caused by alcohol, the obsession with alcohol, and with the destructive behavior as a result of alcohol. The *Big Book*, however, makes this astonishing claim: "Resentment is the 'number one' offender. It destroys more alcoholics than anything else. From it stem all forms of spiritual disease, for we have been not only mentally and physically ill, we have been spiritually sick."[1]

The word *resentment* fundamentally means to "feel again." In other words, when we have resentments, we hold on to a feeling from the past, cling to it, feeling the pain of it over and over again. We may even catch ourself fantasizing about that moment and what we could have done or said. Holding resentments prevents us from being in the present. It is the aching feeling that will not go away. The one sure thing about feelings is that they are not going anywhere unless we do something about them. Resentments are part of life; they do not go away just because alcohol is gone. If we do not address our resentments, we often find ourself right back in the bottle.

In order to relieve resentments, there are a few things we have to do. First, we have to reflect on what our resentments are. Do we resent our boss, our colleagues, our spouse, our parents? We probably hold resentment toward several different people and places. For example: the job for which we were underpaid and underappreciated; our parents for being too controlling or unaffectionate; our spouse for being too judgmental; or even perhaps it is the daily rush-hour traffic.

Next, we have to reflect on why we may have built up these resentments. Did these people, places, or systems have an impact on our self-esteem? Did they threaten our financial security? Did they affect our sexual relations and intimacy? Usually we hold resentments for reasons like these. Our resentments are associated with a fear of losing something that is valuable to us, such as our self-esteem, friendships, lover, or finances.

The most profound work is when we begin our own moral inventory, or in Hebrew, *cheshbon ha-nefesh* (literally, "accounting of the soul"). Here, we honestly confront our own role in contributing to the situation that gave rise to the resentment. For example, perhaps we were overspending and, instead of looking at whether we needed to cut back on our spending, we blamed our job for underpaying us. Or perhaps we were not honest with our spouse about something and she had reason to suspect that something was amiss, yet we blamed her for being judgmental. Or maybe our expectations of others are too great—greater even than our expectations of ourself.

The point is that we have to dig and probe until we get to the origin of the resentment and identify any responsibility we might have for the feeling. By identifying our own part in the situation, we naturally overcome the resentment and gain a more balanced emotional approach to the situation and the people involved. When we do not address and let go of resentments, they mount up in our minds, waiting to manifest into action. Resentments are our warning signs to

eventual sins, reminiscent of God's warning to Cain for being resent-
ful that his brother's offerings were favored over his own:

> *"Why are you distressed,*
> *And why is your face fallen?*
> *Surely if you do right,*
> *There is uplift.*
> *But if you do not do right*
> *Sin couches at the door;*
> *Its urge is toward you,*
> *Yet you can be its master."*
> (Genesis 4:6–7)

In the Jewish text on page 110, Rabbi Abraham Isaac Kook points
out that each sin is correlated with a particular anxiety. That is, when
we sin we are often able to look back and see that we probably could
have avoided the sinful act, which brings a feeling of guilt and anxiety.
Kook and the Jewish tradition offer *teshuvah* as a spiritual mechanism
to heal the sinful act. Step 4 is the work to begin *teshuvah* by unpack-
ing the resentment that may have led to it. It should be noted that
Step 4 work can also preempt a sinful act from occurring in the first
place by early identification of a resentment. In any event, a thorough
cheshbon ha-nefesh, or Step 4 inventory, pinpoints original causes so
that we can pull out the roots of our suffering and replant with seeds
of tranquility.

Step 5

A man of piety complained to the Baal Shem Tov, saying: "I have labored hard and long in service of the Lord, and yet I have received no improvement. I am still an ordinary and ignorant person." The Baal Shem Tov answered: "You have gained the realization that you are ordinary and ignorant, and this in itself is a worthy accomplishment."

—Louis I. Newman, *The Hasidic Anthology*

I t is said that we are only as sick as our secrets. Alcoholics and addicts often weave lies into lifestyle. Much of the lying is buried beneath the omission of the truth. We live with our untold story eating away at us, our soul slowly being crushed under the weight of this burden.

Much of what alcoholics and addicts have done is unacceptable to most and there is legitimate reason to be cautious about whether and who to tell about what we have done. Drinking and using in the morning, driving under the influence, working with clients and even children while we're loaded, infidelity, and thievery may all be part of our story and we feel hopeless shame for it. We feel unforgivable and beyond repair.

But we cannot hold on to our stories forever. We either unload what happened or we die. We die by drinking and using more or we die at our own hands. In any event, we die inside.

The truth is that we cannot tell anyone our story, but we have to tell someone. And we have to tell another alcoholic or addict because another alcoholic or addict will completely understand. In fact, most other alcoholics and addicts have done the same things we have. The liberating truth is that other people suffer from the same pains and have acted out of the pain in similarly destructive ways.

When we tell our stories, we are afraid that our sponsor's jaw will drop in shock and disbelief. But when we finish speaking, the response is always compassion, understanding, or a gentle smile accompanied by the words: "Is that it?"

Undoubtedly, our stories indicate character flaws and defects we must work to improve. They also show us where we need to make amends. Once we have shared our story with another, we are better able to recognize that we are truly not alone and that, although our lives may need to be changed, nothing is insurmountable. We experience the immediate catharsis of relief, and we intuitively know that we can be redeemed. We need not die anymore.

Step 6

"Where is the dwelling of God?"

This was the question with which the rabbi of Kotzk surprised a number of learned men who happened to be visiting him.

They laughed at him: "What a thing to ask! Is not the whole world full of His glory!"

Then he answered his own question: "God dwells wherever man lets him in."

—Louis I. Newman, *The Hasidic Anthology*

Fear. Beneath the resentments, the selfishness, the dishonesty, the blame, and the guilt is this four-letter word that "somehow touches about every aspect of our lives. It was an evil and corroding thread; the fabric of our existence was shot through it."[1] Fear drives us to behave in toxic ways, leading to anger and hatred. There are some who project an aura of self-confidence, but that does not make them fearless. In fact, when self-confidence becomes cockiness or arrogance, fear lurks below.

Fear is with us for a reason. Its function is self-preservation. But we often lose sight of the point when our fears become irrational. We forget or ignore why we might have a particular fear and, in turn, become blind to its irrationality and the pain it is causing in our lives.

One of the most common fears, underlying much of our behavior, is the fear of loss of control of our lives. We dread chaos, especially emotional chaos. So we do things to control it. We might obsess about orderliness and schedules because it gives us a sense of control over our environment. We might obsess about our children—their grades or their performance in sports—because it gives us a sense of control over their lives, and, therefore, our own. We might obsess about our looks and youthfulness, because it gives us a sense of control over how others perceive us.

Drinking and using are also forms of controlling our life and alleviating fear. We control how we feel. We keep ourself safe from feeling emotions of discomfort. We might be uncomfortable about our career, our relationships, our finances, or even about memories from the past, and drinking and using occupy our time, our mind, and our feelings in such a way that we can avoid the discomfort.

Seeking to control our life so that we do not have to face our fears is futile. Eventually, we will have to face them—there truly is no hiding from ourself, as we take us wherever we go. Rather than arranging our lives to avoid facing our fears, we need courage. Courage is the single most important characteristic to living a happy life. Courage should not be confused with calmness during crisis. Courage is not facing a crisis, it is facing ourself—fears and all. Courage is being able to acknowledge when we are fearful and then, despite those fears, do the right thing anyway. Courage is the necessary predecessor to honesty and openness.

In Step 6 we ready ourself to trust God so that we can genuinely pray to overcome our defects. When we try to control our lives, we deny God entrance into our lives by refusing to trust anything but ourself. The truth is that we have very little control over the world. We cannot control nature or other people. We can only control our responses to what life throws our way. We will live better by mustering the courage to allow us to trust in God and we will be able to persevere no matter what situation we encounter.

We are reminded of the quintessential AA prayer, the Serenity Prayer:

> *God grant me the serenity to accept the things I cannot change,*
> *The courage to change the things I can,*
> *And the wisdom to know the difference.*
> *Amen.*

Step 7

Humbly asked Him to remove our shortcomings.

> My God, keep my tongue from evil, my lips from lies.
> Help me ignore those who slander me. Let me be humble
> before all. Open up my heart to Your Torah, that I may
> pursue Your teachings. Frustrate thoughts of evil against
> me; speedily thwart such advice and destroy their schemes.
> Act for the sake of Your compassion, Your power, Your
> holiness, and Your Torah. Answer my prayer for the
> deliverance of Your beloved ones. May the words of my
> mouth and the meditations of my heart be acceptable in
> Your sight, God, my Rock and my Redeemer. May the
> One who brings peace in heaven above bring peace to us
> and to all the people Israel. Amen.
>
> —Concluding meditation in the *Amidah* (the daily prayer)

When we pray our prayers to God, do we expect God to listen to our prayers and fulfill them? Many of us have had a hard time believing that God both hears our prayer and fulfills it because so many prayers go unanswered. Some of us are left unhealed, unredeemed, and unwhole.

So, when we ask God to remove our shortcomings, do we expect God to swoop down from outer space with a celestial dustbuster and suck out our flaws?

That conception of God is not an authentically Jewish one. God is an energy of consciousness that permeates all space and time simultaneously. All space and time, by the way, includes each of us. God is not out there, while we are here. Just as we are in God's image, so is God in our image.

When we pray, we pray to God within ourself. We all have the capacity for good and evil, for divinity and depravity. We are all simultaneously saint and sinner. When we pray, we partner with God, who connects and binds the whole universe and each of us. When we pray honestly, we identify those parts of ourself that rise above the self-centeredness, the voices calling for selfish gratification and self-imposed alienation. And by praying to tap into that healing aspect of ourself, and watching and hearing ourself pray for it, we give ourself permission to release what is blocking our wholeness. We are able to peel away the scaly shells that imprison our heart.

Step 8

Made a list of all persons we had harmed, and became willing to make amends to them all.

> Penitence (*teshuvah*) is inspired by the yearning for all existence to be better, purer, more vigorous and on a higher plane than it is. Within this yearning is a hidden life-force for overcoming every factor that limits and weakens existence.
>
> —Abraham Isaac Kook

The greatest temptation is to give in to the fear that we are all alone, alone and autonomous entities. It is a temptation because to believe we are alone can feed our pride. We can choose to believe that we are solely responsible for all our accomplishments and successes. Of course, we are not. Our accomplishments and successes are the results of gifts we have been given from God, our families, and our environment, such as character traits, material security, and freedom and safety. As Althea Gibson, the tennis great and first black player to play internationally, said: "No matter what accomplishments you achieve, somebody helps you."[1]

On the flip side of taking responsibility for all the good we have, when we give in to the temptation of believing that we are alone and autonomous, we may also begin to think that we do not have to take responsibility for what happens to others. After all, that would make them autonomous entities, too, responsible for their own problems. We might flippantly accuse them of causing their situation themselves, saying: "They made their own choices—they chose their own circumstances." Of course, this is a fallacy, as well. We have an impact on others all the time. Our behavior certainly affects others. So do our attitudes and dispositions. We constantly transmit and share energy with others. We hold each other's energy; we hold each other's pain and shame, as well as joy and optimism.

All we need to do to remind ourselves of this is to observe small children. We can see in their expressions and behavior how much energy—both positive and negative—they absorb from those around them. We can see that they are emotional sponges, reflecting back what others around them are feeling and doing. In this way, we should not deceive ourselves that we are any different as adults than we were as children.

The truth that so many of us seek to deny is that everything is a form of relationship—that we are all connected. And since we are continuously engaged in relationships, we are, at the very least, somewhat responsible for what happens to those around us. Therefore, part of honest, enlightened, and vibrant living is genuinely acknowledging our responsibility for how we have affected and even harmed others.

Step 9

Made direct amends to such people wherever possible, except when to do so would injure them or others.

Sins between man and man; for example, someone who injures a colleague, curses a colleague, steals from him, or the like will never be forgiven until he gives his colleague what he owes him and appeases him. [It must be emphasized that] even if a person restores the money that he owes the wronged person, he must appease him and ask his forgiveness.

Even if a person only upset a colleague by saying certain things, he must appease him and approach him [repeatedly] until he forgives him....

If the wronged party is not appeased, he should repeat the process a second and third time. If he still does not want to forgive him, he may let him alone and does not need to pursue the matter further. On the contrary, the person who refused to grant forgiveness is the one considered as the sinner.

—Maimonides, *Mishneh Torah*, Laws of Repentance 2:9

Alcoholism and addiction are diseases riddled with shame. Shame carries deep emotional and mental anguish and suffering. Shame is rooted in the belief that we are not good enough, smart enough, or good-looking enough. Shame is when we believe that we are unworthy and unlovable. To live with this belief is to live in suffering.

Many of us drink and use because we feel ashamed. Through alcohol and drugs, we seek, either consciously or subconsciously, to relieve that shame. Unfortunately, drinking and using often lead to *shameless* behavior. We lie, we procrastinate, we isolate ourselves, we steal, and we cheat, all to maintain our drinking and using, which keeps us from feeling the suffering related to shame. The tragedy about this shame cycle is that by acting shamelessly in our addiction we become burdened with yet more shame. And then, because of the shame our drinking and using has caused, we often turn to more drinking and using to relieve the continuous suffering of the now-manifold shame.

This sinking spiral of shame is what Dr. Garret O'Connor of Beit T'Shuvah Prevention Center refers to as "malignant shame." And it is this shame that we must abandon in order to heal. But we are not aiming to be shameless. Dr. O'Connor suggests that malignant shame must elevate into motivational shame. That is, while acknowledging shameful acts from the past, we become motivated to do something in order to fix them as best as we can. This is part of the healing process. Step 9 and the process of *teshuvah* call for us to act on that motivational shame and right the wrongs we have committed.

Throughout the 12 Steps, we come to reckon with our past. We see our life and ourself from a different perspective, from God's perspective. And we begin to forgive ourself. Now we are ready to face those we have harmed and say we are sorry. If we have stolen, we make reimbursement. In whatever way we can make amends and appease those we have harmed, we are willing and ready to do it.

Notice, though, that the Jewish tradition places a limit on how much we seek forgiveness and to make amends. It suggests that some people are impossible to appease. We must be ready for such a response without becoming defensive. They have the right to forgive or not to forgive. Judaism wisely pays attention to this situation, saying that we need only ask forgiveness and try to appease someone up to three times. After the third attempt, we are released from the responsibility and the responsibility becomes theirs to forgive or not to forgive.

This is a critical stage of recovery and the climax of the *teshuvah* process. No matter what actual exchange occurs, whether there is immediate forgiveness or understanding, the very fact that we have made sincere attempts to appease those we have harmed is a cleansing and, ultimately, spiritually liberating experience.

Step 10

Continued to take personal inventory and when we were wrong promptly admitted it.

> Rabbi Zusya said: "In the coming world, they will not ask me, 'Why were you not Moses?' They will ask me, 'Why were you not Zusya?'"
>
> —Martin Buber, *Tales of the Hasidim*

One of the common AA mantras is "one day at a time." This is not a statement about counting our days of sobriety. As Dr. Harry Haroutunian of the Betty Ford Center in Palm Springs commonly says: "I have the same amount of sober time as you. One day. From the time I woke up this morning until now." Of course, "Dr. Harry" has more than one day of sobriety (he has years), but his point is that his sobriety demands daily attention—it happens "one day at a time."

The mantra of "one day at a time" also reflects the idea that sobriety does not end once we stop drinking and using. It does not even end once we finish working the Steps. Theoretically, we could complete the Steps in a week's time. Sobriety and healthy spiritual living require daily reflection and continual work. This is the essence of Step 10.

Step 10 encourages us to look at what we have done, what we have thought, and what we have felt during each day, because every single day we are prone to problems, which lead to resentments, grudges, and fears. These will never go away, since they are part of being a human being. As Heschel vehemently expressed: "Here stands a man, and I'll tell you, this is a man who has no problems. Do you know why? He's an idiot!"[1]

To deny our mistakes and imperfections is to deny our humanity. As human beings, we live in the paradox of being more than animals blessed with creative powers. But we are also bound to bodies and the earth, just like animals, with limited creative powers. We are powerful and powerless, helpful and helpless, and we know it.

In this place, the place of unique human existence, between heaven and earth, we will undoubtedly err in frustration, shame, and anger. This tendency to make mistakes is what separates us from the heavens; it is simply who and what we are. Step 10 helps us to accept this about ourself—to accept our imperfections and to accept that we are only expected to be who we are.

We learn in Step 10 that we are imperfect and will make mistakes. We are powerless to achieve perfection. However, we can draw on the powerful side of ourself to heal the pains and to right the wrongs. Since we are imperfect, we have to work at it every day—"one day at a time."

Step 11

Sought through prayer and meditation to improve our conscious contact with God *as we understood Him*, praying only for knowledge of His will for us and the power to carry that out.

> Rabbi Mendel of Kotzk saw to it that his Hasidim [devotees] wore nothing around the neck while praying, "For," he said, "when we speak to God there must be no break between the heart and the brain."
>
> —Maurice Friedman, *A Dialogue with Hasidic Tales*

There are many AA members who describe the experience of dropping to their knees in prayer during a moment of desperation. It is also not uncommon for people to speak of dropping to their knees each night before bed or each morning and asking God for help. Judaism also includes bending knees in prayer every day during several prayers, such as the *Barchu*, the *Amidah*, and the *Aleinu*.

The act of bending or dropping to our knees in prayer is an act of submission, vulnerability, and openness. It is when we yearn to connect with another to the extent that we are willing to let control over life and ourself go. Life can be overwhelming in a flash or it can gradually grow to become overwhelming. If we try to grab the reins and steer life to where we want it, we usually fail. Such attempts are usually of the mind alone, denying feelings and spirit. After all, our mind is proficient at planning and finding solutions and "outs" to the difficulties of life. Yet we will not find the solution in the plans of the mind alone, as the Yiddish proverb says: "Man plans and God laughs."

Prayer is an act of reverence that is of both the mind and the heart. To revere someone or something—or, in this case, God—is to affirm greatness outside of ourself that we admire and respect. What we revere does not have to be perfect, just great. We can revere people, nature, or creative expression. They are manifestations of principles and ideas that inspire us, showing us the power of the spirit and, ultimately, God. But reverence is not just intellectually acknowledging the beauty and integrity of what we revere. Genuine reverence, as opposed to simply being stimulated or impressed, stirs our emotions. Reverence humbles us, as we admire deep spiritual principles actualized in the world through acts of wisdom and compassion, grandeur and beauty, and awesome power. Reverence excites the mind and rouses the heart.

In our world today, reverence is in short supply. We question authority to the point of absurdity. We are skeptical and cynical at first, denying our need to be humbled in reverence. Unfortunately, many of us must crash to our bottom in order to humble ourselves enough to see the good and wise in the world. Step 11, however, encourages us to practice reverence in our daily routine. The more we revere, affirming the greatness, grandeur, and power of the world and the representatives of the spirit, the better we are able to align our will with God's will.

Prayer and meditation may be personal and silent—Judaism teaches that within silence stands wisdom.[1] Prayer and meditation may also be practiced aloud among others. We may practice prayer and meditation in activities that unify soul and body, such as listening to or playing music, artistic expression, engaging with nature, and even exercise. These are different forms of prayer and meditation, yet each is a way to untangle and silence the mind so that we can listen to the heart and soul. Each of these forms of prayerful practice helps open us up, either consciously or not, to the astounding experience of being an independent human being, interconnected with all there is by the spiritual energy of God. The more open we can be to this reality, the more clearly we can see what our place is and what we should be doing in our life.

Step 12

Having had a spiritual awakening as the result of these Steps, we tried to carry this message to alcoholics, and to practice these principles in all our affairs.

> When a learned but ungenerous man asked Rabbi
> Abraham of Stretyn for a drug to attain the fear of God,
> Rabbi Abraham offered him instead one for the love of
> God. "That's even better," cried the man. "Just give it to
> me." "It is the love of one's fellow men," replied the rabbi.
> —Maurice Friedman, *A Dialogue with Hasidic Tales*

The story is told of a non-Jew who wanted to convert to Judaism. He approached the great sage Hillel and asked him to teach him the entire Torah, all of Judaism, in just a minute's time. Hillel answered by paraphrasing a quotation from Leviticus, "Love your neighbor as yourself" (Leviticus 19:18). Hillel said, "That which you hate, do not do to others. That is the entire Torah. The rest is just explanation."[1]

"Love your neighbor as yourself." Of all of the verses in the Torah to reference, why would Hillel choose this one to sum up the entire Torah? Why not a verse about God—perhaps a verse about God as creator or redeemer? Or why not something about being courageous or wise? Why love your neighbor? Hillel teaches us here that the essence of Judaism is the essence of our purpose as human beings—to connect with others.

We are here to connect. We are here to give and to take. In fact, we are constantly giving and taking, whether we are conscious of it or not. The only question is which we are doing now.

As newcomers to AA, as newcomers to spirituality or to a community, we are lost. We are confused and we feel disconnected. We are unable to give as much as we take. We need help. We need a friend, a teacher, a sponsor to make us feel safe, to give us hope, and to provide guidance. There comes a time in recovery, however, when we have learned something and we are no longer newcomers. We have found a nugget, a morsel of truth that nourishes a healthy life and carries us forward. To acquire truth, even if just a kernel, is so inspiring, so invigorating, and so exciting that, when the opportunity arrives, we crave to share it. And we must.

We must share what we have been given and what we have acquired on our own. We must share it and give it away, first of all, because it is not ours to keep. The truth—if it is genuine truth—is universal. The truth, as the Talmud says, "is the seal of God,"[2] and we are merely the vessels that have the honor of transmitting it. None of us owns the truth—it has no patent or title of property—for it was here before us and will remain after us. Second, we must share it because it was given to us. Since it was given to us in trust, we owe it back. Yet, since we cannot return something to someone who already has it, we can only repay our debt by paying it forward. And third, we must share it for our own sake. The paradox of truth and wisdom is that we only keep them by giving them away; we only continue learning them by teaching them to others.

Once we are engaged in spiritual action, the human pitfall is false pride. The temptation is hubris, which is the sanctimonious conceit of our own greatness. Once we fall prey to hubris, complacency sets in and the soul begins to decay. Any good student or good teacher, however, who may certainly know her subject, continues to learn anew with each course. We must learn and relearn, and the only way to continue "to practice these principles in all our affairs" is to continue to learn through sharing, helping, and teaching others.

The practice of sharing, helping, and teaching others is the highest level of connection that we can experience. Indeed, it is the highest form of love, which is the quintessential expression of God. In Judaism, we understand that God demonstrates God's love for us by sharing life with us and "teaching" us how to live a good life through Torah. Parents demonstrate their love by sharing life with their children and teaching them how to live a good life from what they know. And we all demonstrate our love by sharing our lives with others and teaching our truth.

Gratitude

Gratitude is a spiritual state—an energy—comprised of both faith and humility. The faith is of one's own self: that who we are and what we do is of innate worth. The humility is of the recognition that we could not be who we are or do what we do alone and without the help, inspiration, and the faith of others. Gratitude must be expressed through action if it is to become manifest in the world. Here I wish to offer the blessings of gratitude by acknowledging the friends and colleagues who were especially present in my life and in my heart as this work unfolded. Without each of you, my Torah and my soul are not whole.

First, I must acknowledge the tireless work in the field of addiction and Jewish spirituality of Rabbi Abraham J. Twerski and Harriet Rossetto, the authors of this book's foreword and preface, who laid the groundwork for much of what I have learned. They are each an inspiration, prophetic voices in our generation, and I am humbled by their contribution and support.

To my friends, colleagues, and teachers at Beit T'shuvah. Along with Harriet, Rabbi Mark Borovitz, Beit T'Shuvah's senior rabbi, is a hero in the community and his Herculean efforts to heal the broken and redeem the imprisoned is inimitable. Thanks especially to Andy Besser, Shai Blakeney, Dr. Stacey Cohen, Rabbi Gavi Hershoff, Shira Freidlin, Dr. Garrett O'Connor, Matt Shapiro, and Adam Siegel.

To the community of Valley Beth Shalom and all of the clergy, administrators, lay leaders, and teachers. Special thanks to Cantor Phil Baron, Lisa Clumeck, Steve Cohen, Tina Donay, Rabbi Ed Feinstein, Cantor Hershel Fox, Keri Loventhal, Bart Pachino, Rabbi Avi Taff, Michele Warner, and Elana Zimmerman.

To my rabbis and teachers Bradley Shavit Artson and Mimi Feigelson, for being spiritual guides throughout my rabbinic life. And to my former and current AA sponsors who have been models of *menschlikhkite* and love.

Jewish Lights has been gracious and kind throughout the process of creating this book. Thanks to Stuart M. Matlins, founder and publisher, for his incredible wisdom and vision, and for understanding the deep need for attention and spiritual energy devoted to those who suffer with alcoholism and addiction. Also, thanks to my editor, Emily Wichland, vice president of Editorial and Production, for her swift skill and sharp brilliance.

Finally, to my wife, Maureen, and my daughters, Rina, Nili, and Liora. You are the light to my darkness, the hope to my despair, and the courage to my fear. I am in awe of you and I love you.

Glossary of Jewish Terms and Thinkers

Amidah: Literally, "standing." The central Jewish prayer that is said silently while standing. It is also referred to as *Ha-Tefilah* (The Prayer) and as the *Shemoneh Esrei* (Eighteen Blessings).

Aramaic: An ancient Semitic language, closely related to Hebrew. Jews are understood to have adopted Aramaic during the Babylonian exile, thus leading to the use of Aramaic in parts of the Tanakh (e.g., Daniel); the Talmud; and the Zohar. The *Kol Nidre* prayer on the evening of Yom Kippur and the *Kaddish* are in Aramaic.

Aseret Yemei Teshuvah: Literally, "Ten Days of Repentance." A name for the ten days at the beginning of the Hebrew month of Tishrei. The period opens with Rosh Hashanah and concludes with Yom Kippur.

Baal Shem Tov (1698–1760, Ukraine): Yisrael ben Eliezer, known as the Baal Shem Tov ("Master of the Good Name"), is acknowledged as the founder of Hasidism. Most of the biographical information about him is in the form of stories and legends passed down by his disciples. They describe the Baal Shem Tov (also referred to by the acronym *Besht*) as coming from a poor and simple family. His special abilities, related to mysticism, began at an early age, and legend has it that he worked miracles and battled demons. His teachings emphasize spiritual living through joy and through the power and transcendence of prayer.

Bible; the Hebrew Bible: See Tanakh.

Buber, Martin (1878–1965, Austria): Renowned religious philosopher. His translations and organization of Hasidic parables and anecdotes, such as *The Legend of the Baal Shem Tov*, *The Tales of Rabbi Nachman*, and *Tales of the Hasidim*, helped introduce the Western world to Eastern European Jewry. His greatest philosophical discourse is the book *I and Thou*.

Cordovero, Moses ben Jacob (1522–1570, Israel): One of the pre-eminent kabbalists of sixteenth-century Safed. He studied with Joseph Karo and Solomon Alkabetz. Cordovero authored several important kabbalistic works, including *Pardes Rimonim* (Orchard of Pomegranates) and *Tomer Devorah* (Palm Tree of Deborah). His most significant book is *Or Yakar* (Precious Light), which is an extensive commentary on the Zohar and the Torah, among other sacred texts. He is also known by the acronym Ramak.

Gemara: Usually referred to as the Talmud, even though this description is technically erroneous. Written in Aramaic, the Gemara (literally, "Completion") is the discussion of and commentary on the laws of the Mishnah by the rabbinic sages of the second through fifth centuries CE, who are known as *amoraim*. In their explanation and elucidation of the Mishnah, the *amoraim* draw from other sources including the Midrash, the Tosefta, and postbiblical works (e.g., *Ben Sira*, aka *Ecclesiasticus*). Two fifth-century Babylonian sages, Ravina and Rav Ashi, have traditionally been given credit for finalizing the Gemara; modern scholars believe that it did not reach its present form until the end of the seventh century.

Greenberg, Irving "Yitz": The president of the Steinhardt Foundation for Jewish Life. Previously he served as rabbi of the Riverdale Jewish Center in New York City, as an associate professor of history at Yeshiva University, and as founder and chairman of the Department of Jewish Studies at City College of the City University of New York. Rabbi Greenberg was the cofounding president in 1974 of CLAL, the National Center for Learning and Leadership.

halakhah: Literally, "the way"; pl. *halakhot.* Jewish law originating in the Torah and organized by the rabbis in the Mishnah and Talmud.

Hasidim: Literally "Pious Ones." Primarily, this term identifies the followers of Hasidism, the Jewish religious movement founded in the eighteenth century by the Baal Shem Tov.

Heschel, Abraham Joshua (1907–1972, Poland, Germany, USA): One of the great and most widely quoted Jewish religious philosophers in the modern era. Born into a Hasidic family, he studied Talmud in the *Wissenschaft des Judentums* in Germany, and, after escaping the Nazis, he taught at both Hebrew Union College–Jewish Institute of Religion in Cincinnati and The Jewish Theological Seminary. He is also known for being extremely active in the civil rights movement and serving as a leading figure in the Jewish-Christian interfaith movement, which guided the Second Vatican Council. His most famous books are his theological ones, including *The Sabbath, God in Search of Man,* and *Man Is Not Alone.*

Kabbalah: Literally, "Reception." The tradition of Jewish mysticism, which maintains that there are hidden truths in the Torah. The primary resource for Kabbalah is the Zohar. Hasidism is based on many of the teachings of Kabbalah.

kashrut: Literally, "fit" or "proper." The body of Jewish dietary laws dealing with foods, combinations of foods, and how these foods are to be prepared and eaten. The term in English is *kosher,* which is also used to describe objects that are made in accordance with Jewish law and are fit for ritual use.

Kiddush: Literally, "Sanctification." The blessing recited over wine. It is said every Sabbath, on Jewish holidays, and before celebratory meals to sanctify these occasions.

Kook, Abraham Isaac (1865–1935, Israel): Known simply as Rav Kook, he was the first chief rabbi of Israel, while it was still under the British Mandate. He is one of the most important and influential thinkers on religious Zionism in the twentieth century, as well as on Jewish spirituality and law.

Levi Yitzchak of Berditchev (1740–1809, Russia): A revered Hasidic master, he is mentioned in many Hasidic tales and is recognized for his classic work *Kedushat Levi.*

Luria, Isaac (1534–1572, Safed, Israel): A renowned teacher of Kabbalah and *halakhah.* His teachings inspired a school of thought; although Luria himself did not write much, his followers produced volumes of his teachings. Lurianic Kabbalah basically teaches that the purpose of Creation is to have the community and each individual heal the world (*tikkun olam,* literally, "fixing the world"), thus gradually reuniting and perfecting the divine realms (see *sefirah*), as well as humanity.

Luzzatto, Moses Chaim or Ramchal (1707–1747, Italy and Holland): A leading mystic and kabbalist who headed a secret messianic order. Luzzatto authored several kabbalistic writings, including popular volumes, such as *Mesillat Yesharim*, *Migdal Oz*, and *Derech Hashem*. He was a leading supporter of Shabbetai Tzvi, a self-proclaimed messiah who later converted to Islam, and was, therefore, exiled by the Italian rabbinical court. He and his family all died from a plague.

Maimonides/Rambam (1135–1204, Spain and Egypt): Rabbi Moses ben Maimon. A physician and possibly the greatest Jewish thinker of all time. He wrote many important works, including legal codes and philosophical expositions. Among them are the *Mishneh Torah*, the first written Jewish legal code, which is written in remarkably clear Hebrew, and the *Guide of the Perplexed* (*Moreh Nevuchim*), a philosophical work that shows the tremendous influence of Aristotelian philosophy on Maimonides. The *Guide of the Perplexed* interprets the Torah with the objective of eliminating apparent contradictions with philosophy.

Menachem Mendel of Kotzk (1787–1859, Poland): Better known as the Kotzker Rebbe. The Kotzker is considered a Hasidic master with a philosophy of pointed honesty and wit. Many of his sayings are widely quoted in Hasidic tales.

Midrash: Literally, "Elucidation" or "Exposition." A body of work that combines the theological, homiletical, and ethical lore of the Palestinian rabbis from the third through tenth centuries CE. The word *midrash* is derived from the verb root *darash*, which denotes searching out and discovering other meanings and information from Scripture.

Midrash Rabbah: An important series of books that expounds on and further illuminates each book of the Torah, as well as the *megillot* (five historical tales that are part of the biblical book called the Writings): the Song of Songs, Ruth, Esther, Ecclesiastes, and Lamentations. Each volume is identified by the name of the corresponding book from the Bible, followed by the word *rabbah* (meaning "great"), such as Exodus Rabbah and Song of Songs Rabbah. As a series, these works were edited and redacted between the fifth and tenth centuries CE. Final touches to Numbers Rabbah and Esther Rabbah were made as late as the thirteenth century. Genesis Rabbah, the oldest of the series (425 CE), includes material from the Apocrypha, Philo, and Josephus.

minhag: Literally, "custom"; pl. **minhagim.** A custom observed and transmitted by the Jewish people. *Minhagim* often reflect the time and place of the Jews who first kept them. For many people, adherence to Jewish customs can be as strictly maintained as adherence to Jewish law *(halakhah)*.

Mishnah: Literally, "Teaching." The first compilation of the Oral Law and the foundational text for the Talmud and for the rabbinic tradition. Most scholars attribute it to Rabbi Yehudah Ha-Nasi (Rabbi Judah the Patriarch, who lived in Judea under control of the Roman Empire) and date its final editing to circa 200 CE. There are six "orders," or volumes, of the Mishnah, categorized by different areas of Jewish law: *Zera'im* (laws governing agriculture and farm products); *Mo'ed* (laws relating to seasons and holidays); *Nashim* (laws relating to women and family life; marriage and divorce); *Nezikim* (summaries of Jewish civil and criminal law); *Kodashim* (laws relating to holiness in matters of sacrifices and ritual slaughter); and *Toharot* (laws about purity). The word *mishnah* is derived from the verb root meaning "repetition," indicating the primary method for learning and oral study at that time.

mitzvah: Literally, "commandment"; pl. **mitzvot.** One of the religious obligations detailed in the Torah, the majority of which fall into the positive category of religious, ethical, or moral obligations. The Torah also contains negative *mitzvot*, which are prohibitions.

Nachman of Breslov (1772–1810, Ukraine and Russia): One of the most influential and fascinating of all Hasidic rebbes (masters). The great-grandson of the Baal Shem Tov (the founder of Hasidism), Nachman did not believe he was a worthy heir to the leadership of the Hasidic dynasty and chose to embark on a path of deep, and often dark, introspection and self-denial. His teachings and stories were posthumously published in *Likkutei Moharan* (literally, "Collection of Teachings by Our Teacher Rabbi Nachman") and a book of his tales called *Sippurei Ma'asiyot*. They are still widely read.

Nachmanides/Ramban (1194–1270, Spain and Israel): Rabbi Moses ben Nachman, a physician and one of the most important scholars in Jewish history. He is best known for his commentary on the Torah, but he was also an important halakhist, kabbalist, and poet. Between 1263 and 1265, he represented Spanish Jewry in an official debate between Christians and Jews about religious truths.

rabbis, the: The leaders of rabbinic Judaism. The time of greatest rabbinic development occurred when rabbinic Judaism evolved to become normative Judaism. The first division of this era was that of the sages. These sages were called *tannaim*, a word that comes from the Aramaic word for "repeat," for which the Aramaic root T-N-H is equivalent to the Hebrew root S-N-H. That Hebrew root is also the basis for the word *Mishnah* (Oral Law); thus the *tannaim* were "Mishnah teachers" who repeated and passed down the Oral Torah. Most of the *tannaim* lived in the period between the destruction of the Second Temple (70 CE) and the Bar Kochba Revolt (135 CE). The second division of the rabbinic era is that of the *amoraim*, a word that comes from the Aramaic word for "speaker." The *amoraim* continued to interpret and transmit Jewish law, thought, and practice, expanding on the foundations laid by the *tannaim*. This work was carried out at academies in Palestine (Tiberias, Caesarea, and Tzippori) and in Babylonia (Nehardea, Pumpedita, and Sura). The Talmud, which was primarily compiled about 400 CE in Palestine and about 500 CE in Babylonia, provides the fullest expression of the *amoraim*.

Rashi (1040–1105, France): Rabbi Shlomo ben Yitzchak. Generally regarded as the greatest commentator on both the Torah and the Talmud. Without his explanations, both would be much more difficult to understand. His commentary on the Torah was the first book to be printed in Hebrew; the semicursive typeface, which the printer created to distinguish the explanations from the biblical text, is called "Rashi script" and is still used today.

Rosenzweig, Franz (1886–1929, Germany): Influential Jewish philosopher. After a life-changing experience on Yom Kippur, Rosenzweig reaffirmed his Jewish identity and turned to Jewish philosophy, becoming a student of Hermann Cohen and a friend of Martin Buber.

Rosh Hashanah: Literally, "Head of the Year." The Jewish New Year. It falls on the first and second days of Tishrei, the seventh Hebrew month (in September or October). Rosh Hashanah always falls on the Rosh Hodesh (new moon) that is closest to the autumnal equinox.

sages: A descriptive term to indicate those rabbis who contributed the greatest insights and developments in Jewish thought and practice. Most references in this book are to rabbis of the rabbinic era, but there are several rabbis from the medieval period (for example, Nachmanides) for whom the term is also used.

Salanter, Israel (1810–1883, Lithuania and Germany): Known as the father of the Mussar Movement. In Mussar, Salanter emphasized dedication to the study of upright living over purely academic endeavors in talmudic study. His teachings, especially those pertaining to psychological concepts, influenced many subsequent rabbis and teachers.

Schulweis, Harold M.: The longtime spiritual leader of Congregation Valley Beth Shalom in Encino, California. He holds a master's degree in philosophy from New York University and was ordained at the Jewish Theological Seminary. Rabbi Schulweis has authored several books, including *For Those Who Can't Believe, Approach to the Philosophy of Religion, Evil and the Morality of God*, and *In God's Mirror*.

sefirah: Literally, "portion"; pl. ***sefirot.*** One of the ten emanations, or varying aspects, of God in the universe. The *sefirot* play a central role throughout kabbalistic doctrine and teachings. Each *sefirah* embodies a divine quality and, according to Kabbalah, the *sefirot* are the underlying forces in the world and in the Torah.

Shabbat; pl. Shabbatot: The Sabbath, or day of rest. It begins at sunset on Friday night and ends about twenty-five hours later, after sunset on Saturday night. (The extra hour ensures that the full twenty-four-hour period is observed.)

shofar; pl. ***shofarot:*** The ram's horn that is sounded during the month of Elul, on Rosh Hashanah, and at the end of Yom Kippur. It is mentioned numerous times in the Bible, in reference to its ceremonial use in the Temple and to its function as a signal-horn of war.

simchah: Literally, "joy" or "happiness"; pl. *s'machot.* A joyous celebration, such as a wedding or bar mitzvah.

Talmud: The central and most important body of rabbinic literature. Combining the Mishnah and Gemara, the Talmud contains material from the rabbinic academies that date from sometime before the second century CE through the sixth century CE. It includes *halakhic* and midrashic expositions, wisdom, personal stories, and arguments. There are two versions: the Jerusalem (*Yerushalmi*) or Palestinian Talmud and the Babylonian (*Bavli*) Talmud. When people speak of the Talmud generically, they are referring to the *Bavli*, as it is more extensive and more widely used. There are sixty-three areas of study that make up the Talmud, called tractates (*masechtot*). The Talmud serves as the primary source for all later codes of Jewish law.

Tanakh: An acronym for the three books that make up the cornerstone of Jewish beliefs comprising Torah (the Five Books of Moses), Nevi'im (Prophets), and Ketuvim (Writings). When Jews speak of the Bible, they are referring to the Tanakh.

teshuvah: Literally, "return." Referring to the "return to God," *teshuvah* is often translated as "repentance." It is one of the most significant themes and spiritual components of the High Holidays.

Yom Kippur: Literally, "Day of Atonement." The most holy and solemn day of the Jewish calendar, filled with pleas for forgiveness and acts of self-denial, including fasting. It falls on the tenth day of the Hebrew month of Tishrei, which is usually late September or early October.

Zusya, Meshulam (1718–1800, Poland): A Hasidic great, Reb Zusya is commonly mentioned in Hasidic tales about the early founders of Hasidism.

Notes

Part I: A Judaism of Experience, Strength, and Hope

1. Bill Wilson, *The AA Way of Life: A Reader by Bill* (New York: Alcoholics Anonymous World Services, 1967), p. 323.
2. Abraham Joshua Heschel, *Who Is Man?* (Palo Alto, Calif.: Stanford University Press, 1965), p. 87.

Chapter 1: Understanding Addiction, Jewish Spirituality, and Medicine

1. Mishnah, *Avot* 4:1.
2. Harry Haroutunian, *Being Sober* (New York: Rodale Books, 2013), p. 6. See also A. C. Heath, K. K. Bucholz, P. A. Madden, et al. "Genetic and Environmental Contributions to Alcohol Dependence Risk in a National Twin Sample: Consistency of Findings in Women and Men," *Psychological Medicine* 27, no. 6 (1997): 1381–1396; and M. McGue, "The Behavioral Genetics of Alcoholism," *Current Directions in Psychological Science* 8 (1999): 109–115.
3. See the film *Pleasure Unwoven: An Explanation of the Brain Disease of Addiction*, directed by Kevin McCauley and produced by Jim Clegg (Institute for Addiction Study, 2010).
4. B. Talmud, *Sanhedrin* 91b.
5. *Mishneh Torah,* Laws of Proper Behavior 3:2, 3:3, and 4:15.

Chapter 2: A God of Religion and Recovery

1. *Alcoholics Anonymous: The Story of How More Than One Hundred Men Have Recovered from Alcoholism*. (New York: Works Publishing, 1939), pp. 567.
2. B. Talmud, *Berakhot* 26b. The Talmud here claims that each of the three patriarchs prayed to God and related to the Divine at three different times of the day, thereby establishing the thrice-daily times for prayer: morning, afternoon, and evening.
3. Martin Buber, *Ten Rungs: Collected Hasidic Sayings* (London: Routledge Press, 1947; reprint ed. 2002), pp. 15–16.

4. Mishnah, *Avot* 2:4.

5. Buber, *Ten Rungs*, p. 55.

6. See also Maimonides, *Introduction to Commentary on Mishnah Avot, Shemonah Perakim*.

7. See Jeremy Kalmanofsky, "Faithful and Sane," *Judaism* (Summer–Fall, 2005): 173–177.

8. Franz Rosenzweig and Nahum Glatzer, *Franz Rosenzweig: His Life and Thought* (New York: Hachette Publishing, 1961; reprint ed. 1998), p. 206.

Chapter 3: The Dignity of the Self

1. Irving Greenberg, "Seeking the Roots of Religious Pluralism," *Journal of Ecumenical Studies,* no. 3 (1997): 386–387. Erich Fromm also points out this question and uses the same proof text. See Erich Fromm, *And You Shall Be As Gods* (New York: Holt, Rinehart, and Winston, 1966), pp. 82–84.

2. Mishnah, *Sanhedrin* 4:5.

3. See Rashi on Gen. 6:9.

4. Midrash, Numbers Rabbah 13:15.

5. Nachmanides, commentary on Leviticus 19:2.

6. "The Twelve Traditions," Tradition #11. See *Alcoholics Anonymous*, p. 562.

7. *Alcoholics Anonymous*, p. 17.

8. Rabbi Brous broadcasts some of her classes from the podcast *Ikar of Judaism.*

9. Midrash, Exodus Rabbah 5:9.

10. See Charles K. Bellinger, *The Genealogy of Violence: Reflections on Creation, Freedom, and Evil* (Oxford: Oxford University Press, 2001), p. 65.

Chapter 4: The Evil Inclination

1. Erich Fromm, *Man for Himself* (New York: Holt, Rinehart, and Winston, 1947), p. 20.

2. Midrash, Genesis Rabbah 9:7. Even death is considered to be good, according to another midrash; see Midrash, Genesis Rabbah 9:5.

3. Midrash, Leviticus Rabbah 4:6.

4. Midrash, Genesis Rabbah 9:7.

5. Midrash, *Sifra* on Leviticus 20:26.

6. Mishnah, *Avot* 4:1.

7. *Twelve Steps and Twelve Traditions* (New York: Alcoholics Anonymous World Services, 1953, reprint ed. 2012), p. 45.

8. Maurice Friedman, *A Dialogue with Hasidic Tales: Hallowing the Everyday* (New York: Human Sciences Press, 1988), p. 39.

9. *Twelve Steps and Twelve Traditions,* pp. 45–46.

10. B. Talmud, *Sukkah* 52b.

11. E. Kurtz and K. Ketchum, *The Spirituality of Imperfection* (New York: Bantam Books, 1992), pp. 189–190.

12. Israel Salanter, *Ohr Yisrael*, trans. Tzvi Miller (Southfield, Mich.: Targum, 2004), p. 399.

13. Moses Chaim Luzzatto, *The Way of God,* vol. 1, trans. by Aryeh Kaplan (New York: Feldheim Publishers, 1997), p. 45.

14. Friedman, *A Dialogue with Hasidic Tales,* p. 40.

Chapter 5: Judaism and Alcohol

1. *Alcoholics Anonymous*, pp. 30–31.

2. *Narcotics Anonymous*, 5th ed. (Chatsworth, Calif.: Narcotics Anonymous World Services, 2000), p. 15.

3. Kelly Hartog, "Just Say No, Even on Purim," *Jewish Journal of Greater Los Angeles* (March 18, 2005), www.ou.org/holidays/purim/just-say-even-purim. I have personal knowledge of Chabad houses in several communities where teens are promised liquor if they come in for Purim or Simchat Torah. Furthermore, online blogs record many angry parents discussing this exact problem; see, for example, orthomom.blogspot.com/2006/03/more-on-purim-and-underage-drinking.html.

4. Leviticus 10:8–11.

5. Numbers 6:1–8.

6. Kalonymous Kalman Shapiro, *Conscious Community*, trans. by Andrea Cohen Kiener (Northvale, N.J.: Aronson Press, 1977), p. 95.

7. *Alcoholics Anonymous*, p. 28.

8. Louis I. Newman, ed., *The Hasidic Anthology* (Northvale, N.J.: Jason Aronson, 1963), p. 42. Although the word *laughing* is not used, there are references to *happy to be alive* and *cheerful without cause*. Nonetheless, I have heard this sequence offered orally by various teachers, who included *laughing* as the third lesson.

9. Paul Steinberg, *Celebrating the Jewish Year: The Winter Holidays* (Philadelphia: Jewish Publication Society, 2007), pp. 123ff.

10. B. Talmud, *Megillah* 7b.
11. Alexander Ziskind, *The Foundation and Root of Worship (Yesod v'Shoresh ha-Avodah)*, as discussed by Rabbi Tzvi Hersh Weinreb, March 15, 2005, in a press release from the Orthodox Union: "It Is *Not* a Mitzvah to Get Drunk on Purim!"
12. *Be'ur Halakhah* on the Mishnah, *Berurah* 695:2.
13. B. Talmud, *Megillah* 7b.

Part II: The Covenant of Recovery

1. *Alcoholics Anonymous*, p. 83.
2. *Narcotics Anonymous*, 5th ed., p. 18.

Chapter 6: Study—*Talmud Torah*

1. B. Talmud, *Shabbat* 127a.
2. See Rashi on Genesis 1:14 (Midrash, Genesis Rabbah 3:6; and B. Talmud, *Pesachim* 2a and *Chagigah* 12a). See also Midrash, Genesis Rabbah 9:14; and Midrash, *Pesikta Rabbati*, *Hosafah* 2:1.
3. B. Talmud, *Bava Kamma* 83ff.
4. B. Talmud, *Sanhedrin* 71a.
5. *Degel Mahaneh Efraim*, *Bereishit* (Jerusalem: 1963), pp. 5b–6a.
6. Mishnah, *Avot* 1:6 and 1:16.
7. Martin Buber, *Tales of the Hasidim: The Early Masters* (New York: Schocken, 1947), p. 256.

Chapter 7: Prayer—*Tefilah*

1. The quotation from the Sabbath liturgy is: *v'taheir libeinu le'avdekha be'emet*. I amended Heschel's translation of the prayer slightly so that it resounds in more contemporary language. I translated the Hebrew *oved* as "serve" as opposed to his "worship" and I changed his word *Thee* to *You*.
2. While Rabbi Schulweis said this to me directly, he has written something similar in "Fear of Death": "Fear—not of death or dying but of not having lived." This poem can be found in Harold Schulweis, *Finding Each Other in Judaism: Meditations on the Rites of Passage from Birth to Immortality* (New York: UAHC Press, 2001), p. 92.
3. Mishnah, *Avot* 1:14.

4. From a 1972 interview with Carl Stern on the NBC broadcast *Eternal Light*. See interview transcript at www.philosophy-religion.org/religion_links/aj_heschel.htm.

5. Quoted in *A Treasury of Thoughts on Jewish Prayer*, ed. Sidney Greenberg (Northvale, N.J.: Jason Aronson, 1989), p. 158.

Chapter 8: Repentance—*Teshuvah*

1. Quoted in *Hasidic Wisdom: Sayings from the Jewish Sages*, ed. Simcha Raz, trans. Dov Peretz Elkins and Jonathan Elkins (Northvale, N.J.: Jason Aronson, 1997), p. 74.

2. B. Talmud, *Nedarim* 39b.

3. B. Talmud, *Yoma* 86a.

4. *Alcoholics Anonymous*, p. 75.

5. Abraham Isaac Kook, *The Lights of Return*, trans. Alter B. Z. Metzger (New York: Yeshiva University, 1978), p. 30.

6. B. Talmud, *Berakhot* 34b.

Chapter 9: Service—*Tikkun*

1. See Mishnah, *Gittin* 4:2.

2. Abraham Isaac Kook, *Orot Ha-Kodesh* (Jerusalem: Mossad HaRav Kook, 1985), sect. 3, p. 180.

3. Parker Palmer, *The Politics of the Brokenhearted* (Kalamazoo, MI: Fetzer Institute, 2005), p. 232. Accessed online at www.fetzer.org/sites/default/files/images/resources/attachment/2012-07-12/dad_palmer_essay.pdf.

4. See Deuteronomy 10:16, 30:6; and Jeremiah 4:4.

5. As told by Jacob Needleman, found in Parker Palmer, *Healing the Heart of Democracy* (San Francisco: Jossey Bass, 2001), pp. 149–150.

6. *Avot de Rabbi Natan* 4:5.

7. *Alcoholics Anonymous*, p. 89.

8. Martin Buber, *Israel and the World: Essays in a Time of Crisis* (New York: Schocken Books, 1948), p. 145.

Part III: 12 Texts for the 12 Steps

1. *Alcoholics Anonymous*, pp. 83–84.

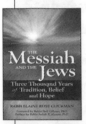

Meditation

The Magic of Hebrew Chant
Healing the Spirit, Transforming the Mind, Deepening Love
By Rabbi Shefa Gold; Foreword by Sylvia Boorstein
Introduces this transformative spiritual practice as a way to unlock the power of sacred texts and make prayer and meditation the delight of your life. Includes musical notations.
6 x 9, 352 pp, Quality PB, 978-1-58023-671-3 **$24.99**

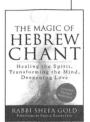

The Magic of Hebrew Chant Companion—The Big Book of Musical Notations
and Incantations
8½ x 11, 154 pp, PB, 978-1-58023-722-2 **$19.99**

Jewish Meditation Practices for Everyday Life
Awakening Your Heart, Connecting with God
By Rabbi Jeff Roth
Offers a fresh take on meditation that draws on life experience and living life with greater clarity as opposed to the traditional method of rigorous study.
6 x 9, 224 pp, Quality PB, 978-1-58023-397-2 **$18.99**

Discovering Jewish Meditation, 2nd Edition
Instruction & Guidance for Learning an Ancient Spiritual Practice
By Nan Fink Gefen, PhD 6 x 9, 208 pp, Quality PB, 978-1-58023-462-7 **$16.99**

The Handbook of Jewish Meditation Practices
A Guide for Enriching the Sabbath and Other Days of Your Life
By Rabbi David A. Cooper 6 x 9, 208 pp, Quality PB, 978-1-58023-102-2 **$16.95**

Meditation from the Heart of Judaism
Today's Teachers Share Their Practices, Techniques, and Faith
Edited by Avram Davis 6 x 9, 256 pp, Quality PB, 978-1-58023-049-0 **$18.99**

Spirituality / Women's Interest

New Jewish Feminism
Probing the Past, Forging the Future
Edited by Rabbi Elyse Goldstein; Foreword by Anita Diamant
Looks at the growth and accomplishments of Jewish feminism and what they mean for Jewish women today and tomorrow.
6 x 9, 480 pp, HC, 978-1-58023-359-0 **$24.99**

The Divine Feminine in Biblical Wisdom Literature
Selections Annotated & Explained
Translation & Annotation by Rabbi Rami Shapiro
5½ x 8½, 240 pp, Quality PB, 978-1-59473-109-9 **$16.99***

The Quotable Jewish Woman
Wisdom, Inspiration & Humor from the Mind & Heart
Edited by Elaine Bernstein Partnow
6 x 9, 496 pp, Quality PB, 978-1-58023-236-4 **$19.99**

The Women's Haftarah Commentary
New Insights from Women Rabbis on the 54 Weekly Haftarah Portions, the 5 Megillot & Special Shabbatot
Edited by Rabbi Elyse Goldstein
Illuminates the historical significance of female portrayals in the Haftarah and the Five Megillot.
6 x 9, 560 pp, Quality PB, 978-1-58023-371-2 **$19.99**

The Women's Torah Commentary
New Insights from Women Rabbis on the 54 Weekly Torah Portions
Edited by Rabbi Elyse Goldstein
Over fifty women rabbis offer inspiring insights on the Torah, in a week-by-week format.
6 x 9, 496 pp, Quality PB, 978-1-58023-370-5 **$19.99**; HC, 978-1-58023-076-6 **$34.95**

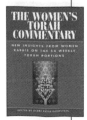

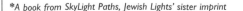

*A book from SkyLight Paths, Jewish Lights' sister imprint

Inspiration

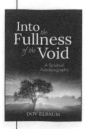

Into the Fullness of the Void: A Spiritual Autobiography *By Dov Elbaum*
The spiritual autobiography of one of Israel's leading cultural figures that provides insights and guidance for all of us. 6 x 9, 304 pp, Quality PB Original, 978-1-58023-715-4 **$18.99**

Saying No and Letting Go: Jewish Wisdom on Making Room for What Matters Most
By Rabbi Edwin Goldberg, DHL; Foreword by Rabbi Naomi Levy
Taps into timeless Jewish wisdom that teaches how to "hold on tightly" to the things that matter most while learning to "let go lightly" of the demands and worries that do not ultimately matter. 6 x 9, 192 pp, Quality PB, 978-1-58023-670-6 **$16.99**

The Bridge to Forgiveness: Stories and Prayers for Finding God and Restoring Wholeness *By Rabbi Karyn D. Kedar* 6 x 9, 176 pp, Quality PB, 978-1-58023-451-1 **$16.99**

The Empty Chair: Finding Hope and Joy—Timeless Wisdom from a Hasidic Master, Rebbe Nachman of Breslov *Adapted by Moshe Mykoff and the Breslov Research Institute*
4 x 6, 128 pp, Deluxe PB w/ flaps, 978-1-879045-67-5 **$9.99**

A Formula for Proper Living: Practical Lessons from Life and Torah
By Rabbi Abraham J. Twerski, MD 6 x 9, 144 pp, HC, 978-1-58023-402-3 **$19.99**

The Gentle Weapon: Prayers for Everyday and Not-So-Everyday Moments—Timeless Wisdom from the Teachings of the Hasidic Master, Rebbe Nachman of Breslov *Adapted by Moshe Mykoff and S. C. Mizrahi, together with the Breslov Research Institute*
4 x 6, 144 pp, Deluxe PB w/ flaps, 978-1-58023-022-3 **$9.99**

The God Upgrade: Finding Your 21st-Century Spirituality in Judaism's 5,000-Year-Old Tradition *By Rabbi Jamie Korngold; Foreword by Rabbi Harold M. Schulweis*
6 x 9, 176 pp, Quality PB, 978-1-58023-443-6 **$15.99**

God Whispers: Stories of the Soul, Lessons of the Heart *By Rabbi Karyn D. Kedar*
6 x 9, 176 pp, Quality PB, 978-1-58023-088-9 **$16.99**

God's To-Do List: 103 Ways to Be an Angel and Do God's Work on Earth
By Dr. Ron Wolfson 6 x 9, 144 pp, Quality PB, 978-1-58023-301-9 **$16.99**

Happiness and the Human Spirit: The Spirituality of Becoming the Best You Can Be
By Rabbi Abraham J. Twerski, MD
6 x 9, 176 pp, Quality PB, 978-1-58023-404-7 **$16.99**; HC, 978-1-58023-343-9 **$19.99**

Life's Daily Blessings: Inspiring Reflections on Gratitude and Joy for Every Day, Based on Jewish Wisdom *By Rabbi Kerry M. Olitzky* 4½ x 6½, 368 pp, Quality PB, 978-1-58023-396-5 **$16.99**

The Magic of Hebrew Chant: Healing the Spirit, Transforming the Mind, Deepening Love *By Rabbi Shefa Gold; Foreword by Sylvia Boorstein*
6 x 9, 352 pp, Quality PB, 978-1-58023-671-3 **$24.99**

Restful Reflections: Nighttime Inspiration to Calm the Soul, Based on Jewish Wisdom *By Rabbi Kerry M. Olitzky and Rabbi Lori Forman-Jacobi* 4½ x 6½, 448 pp, Quality PB, 978-1-58023-091-9 **$16.99**

Sacred Intentions: Morning Inspiration to Strengthen the Spirit, Based on Jewish Wisdom *By Rabbi Kerry M. Olitzky and Rabbi Lori Forman-Jacobi* 4½ x 6½, 448 pp, Quality PB, 978-1-58023-061-2 **$16.99**

The Seven Questions You're Asked in Heaven: Reviewing and Renewing Your Life on Earth *By Dr. Ron Wolfson* 6 x 9, 176 pp, Quality PB, 978-1-58023-407-8 **$16.99**

Kabbalah / Mysticism

Ehyeh: A Kabbalah for Tomorrow
By Rabbi Arthur Green, PhD 6 x 9, 224 pp, Quality PB, 978-1-58023-213-5 **$18.99**

The Gift of Kabbalah: Discovering the Secrets of Heaven, Renewing Your Life on Earth
By Tamar Frankiel, PhD 6 x 9, 256 pp, Quality PB, 978-1-58023-141-1 **$18.99**

Jewish Mysticism and the Spiritual Life: Classical Texts, Contemporary Reflections *Edited by Dr. Lawrence Fine, Dr. Eitan Fishbane and Rabbi Or N. Rose*
6 x 9, 256 pp, HC, 978-1-58023-434-4 **$24.99**; Quality PB, 978-1-58023-719-2 **$18.99**

Seek My Face: A Jewish Mystical Theology *By Rabbi Arthur Green, PhD*
6 x 9, 304 pp, Quality PB, 978-1-58023-130-5 **$19.95**

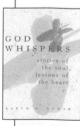

Zohar: Annotated & Explained *Translation & Annotation by Dr. Daniel C. Matt; Foreword by Andrew Harvey* 5½ x 8½, 176 pp, Quality PB, 978-1-893361-51-5 **$18.99**
(A book from SkyLight Paths, Jewish Lights' sister imprint)

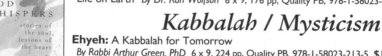

Twelve Steps

Recovery—The Sacred Art
The Twelve Steps as Spiritual Practice
By Rami Shapiro; Foreword by Joan Borysenko, PhD
Draws on insights and practices of different religious traditions to help you move more deeply into the universal spirituality of the Twelve Step system.
5½ x 8½, 240 pp, Quality PB Original, 978-1-59473-259-1 **$16.99***

100 Blessings Every Day: Daily Twelve Step Recovery Affirmations, Exercises for
Personal Growth & Renewal Reflecting Seasons of the Jewish Year
By Rabbi Kerry M. Olitzky; Foreword by Rabbi Neil Gillman, PhD
4½ x 6¼, 432 pp, Quality PB, 978-1-879045-30-9 **$18.99**

Recovery from Codependence: A Jewish Twelve Steps Guide to Healing Your Soul
By Rabbi Kerry M. Olitzky
6 x 9, 160 pp, Quality PB, 978-1-879045-32-3 **$13.95**

Twelve Jewish Steps to Recovery, 2nd Edition: A Personal Guide to Turning
from Alcoholism & Other Addictions—Drugs, Food, Gambling, Sex...
By Rabbi Kerry M. Olitzky and Stuart A. Copans, MD; Preface by Abraham J. Twerski, MD
6 x 9, 160 pp, Quality PB, 978-1-58023-409-2 **$16.99**

Grief / Healing

Judaism and Health
A Handbook of Practical, Professional and Scholarly Resources
Edited by Jeff Levin, PhD, MPH, and Michele F. Prince, LCSW, MAJCS
Foreword by Rabbi Elliot N. Dorff, PhD
Explores the expressions of health in the form of overviews of research studies, first-person narratives and advice.
6 x 9, 448 pp, HC, 978-1-58023-714-7 **$50.00**

Facing Illness, Finding God: How Judaism Can Help You and Caregivers Cope
When Body or Spirit Fails   *By Rabbi Joseph B. Meszler*
6 x 9, 208 pp, Quality PB, 978-1-58023-423-8 **$16.99**

Grief in Our Seasons: A Mourner's Kaddish Companion   *By Rabbi Kerry M. Olitzky*
4½ x 6½, 448 pp, Quality PB, 978-1-879045-55-2 **$18.99**

Healing and the Jewish Imagination: Spiritual and Practical Perspectives on
Judaism and Health   *Edited by Rabbi William Cutter, PhD*
6 x 9, 240 pp, Quality PB, 978-1-58023-373-6 **$19.99**

Healing from Despair: Choosing Wholeness in a Broken World
By Rabbi Elie Kaplan Spitz with Erica Shapiro Taylor; Foreword by Abraham J. Twerski, MD
5½ x 8½, 208 pp, Quality PB, 978-1-58023-436-8 **$16.99**

Healing of Soul, Healing of Body: Spiritual Leaders Unfold the Strength & Solace
in Psalms   *Edited by Rabbi Simkha Y. Weintraub, LCSW*
6 x 9, 128 pp, 2-color illus. text, Quality PB, 978-1-879045-31-6 **$16.99**

Midrash & Medicine: Healing Body and Soul in the Jewish Interpretive Tradition
Edited by Rabbi William Cutter, PhD; Foreword by Michele F. Prince, LCSW, MAJCS
6 x 9, 352 pp, Quality PB, 978-1-58023-484-9 **$21.99**

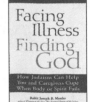

Mourning & Mitzvah, 2nd Edition: A Guided Journal for Walking the Mourner's
Path through Grief to Healing   *By Rabbi Anne Brener, LCSW*
7½ x 9, 304 pp, Quality PB, 978-1-58023-113-8 **$19.99**

Tears of Sorrow, Seeds of Hope, 2nd Edition: A Jewish Spiritual Companion
for Infertility and Pregnancy Loss   *By Rabbi Nina Beth Cardin*
6 x 9, 208 pp, Quality PB, 978-1-58023-233-3 **$18.99**

A Time to Mourn, a Time to Comfort, 2nd Edition: A Guide to Jewish
Bereavement   *By Dr. Ron Wolfson; Foreword by Rabbi David J. Wolpe*
7 x 9, 384 pp, Quality PB, 978-1-58023-253-1 **$21.99**

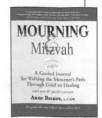

When a Grandparent Dies: A Kid's Own Remembering Workbook for Dealing
with Shiva and the Year Beyond   *By Nechama Liss-Levinson, PhD*
8 x 10, 48 pp, 2-color text, HC, 978-1-879045-44-6 **$15.95** *For ages 7–13*

About Jewish Lights

People of all faiths and backgrounds yearn for books that attract, engage, educate, and spiritually inspire.

Our principal goal is to stimulate thought and help all people learn about who the Jewish People are, where they come from, and what the future can be made to hold. While people of our diverse Jewish heritage are the primary audience, our books speak to people in the Christian world as well and will broaden their understanding of Judaism and the roots of their own faith.

We bring to you authors who are at the forefront of spiritual thought and experience. While each has something different to say, they all say it in a voice that you can hear.

Our books are designed to welcome you and then to engage, stimulate, and inspire. We judge our success not only by whether or not our books are beautiful and commercially successful, but by whether or not they make a difference in your life.

For your information and convenience, at the back of this book we have provided a list of other Jewish Lights books you might find interesting and useful. They cover all the categories of your life:

Bar/Bat Mitzvah	Life Cycle
Bible Study / Midrash	Meditation
Children's Books	Men's Interest
Congregation Resources	Parenting
Current Events / History	Prayer / Ritual / Sacred Practice
Ecology / Environment	Social Justice
Fiction: Mystery, Science Fiction	Spirituality
Grief / Healing	Theology / Philosophy
Holidays / Holy Days	Travel
Inspiration	Twelve Steps
Kabbalah / Mysticism / Enneagram	Women's Interest

Stuart M. Matlins, Publisher

Or phone, fax, mail or email to: **JEWISH LIGHTS Publishing**
Sunset Farm Offices, Route 4 • P.O. Box 237 • Woodstock, Vermont 05091
Tel: (802) 457-4000 • Fax: (802) 457-4004 • www.jewishlights.com
Credit card orders: **(800) 962-4544** (8:30AM–5:30PM EST Monday–Friday)
Generous discounts on quantity orders. SATISFACTION GUARANTEED. Prices subject to change.